Summer of Soul (... Or, When the Revolution Could Not Be Televised)

The fifth title in the Docalogue series, this book examines Ahmir "Questlove" Thompson's 2021 documentary, *Summer of Soul (... Or, When the Revolution Could Not Be Televised)*.

The award-winning film draws on archival footage and interviews to examine the legacy of the Harlem Cultural Festival, a showcase of Black music staged weekly throughout the summer of 1969. The film interrogates this event as a piece of "forgotten" history and prompts critical reflection on why this history was lost while also raising important questions related to archival preservation and cultural memory. Combining five different perspectives, this book acts both as an intensive scholarly treatment and as a pedagogical guide for how to analyze, theorize, and contextualize a documentary. Together, the chapters in this book touch upon key topics related to the study of popular music, musical performance, and audiences; the discovery and reuse of archives and archival documents; and Black studies and American cultural history more broadly.

This book will be of interest to students and scholars in multiple areas, including but not limited to archival studies, Black studies, cultural studies, documentary studies, historiography, and music studies.

Jaimie Baron teaches film and media at the University of California, Berkeley, USA. She is a media scholar and the author of two books of media theory, *The Archive Effect: Found Footage and the Audiovisual Experience of History* (2014) and *Reuse, Misuse, Abuse: The Ethics of Audiovisual Appropriation in the Digital Era* (2020), as well as numerous journal articles and book chapters. She is also the director of the Festival of (In)appropriation, a yearly international festival of short experimental found footage films and videos.

Kristen Fuhs is Professor of Media Studies at Woodbury University, USA. She writes about documentary film, the American criminal justice system, and contemporary celebrity, and her work has appeared in journals such as *Cultural Studies*; the *Historical Journal of Film, Radio, and Television*; and the *Journal of Sport & Social Issues*.

Docalogue

Each book in the Docalogue book series highlights a recent documentary film from five different scholarly perspectives. By focusing on a single documentary from multiple points of view, each book demonstrates the ways in which a single film can open onto diverse questions having to do with the status of the "real," documentary ethics, and the politics of representation, among other issues. The book series is an extension of Docalogue.com, a monthly online publication that consists of short essays about contemporary documentary films.

Series Editors: Jaimie Baron and Kristen Fuhs

I Am Not Your Negro
A Docalogue
Edited by Jaimie Baron and Kristen Fuhs

Kedi
A Docalogue
Edited by Jaimie Baron and Kristen Fuhs

Tiger King
A Docalogue
Edited by Jaimie Baron and Kristen Fuhs

Honeyland
A Docalogue
Edited by Jaimie Baron and Kristen Fuhs

Summer of Soul (. . . Or, When the Revolution Could Not Be Televised)
A Docalogue
Edited by Jaimie Baron and Kristen Fuhs

For more information on the series, visit: www.routledge.com/Docalogue/book-series/ DOCALOGUE

Summer of Soul (... Or, When the Revolution Could Not Be Televised)
A Docalogue

Edited by Jaimie Baron and Kristen Fuhs

First published 2024
by Routledge
605 Third Avenue, New York, NY 10158

and by Routledge
4 Park Square, Milton Park, Abingdon, Oxon, OX14 4RN

Routledge is an imprint of the Taylor & Francis Group, an informa business

© 2024 selection and editorial matter, Jaimie Baron and Kristen Fuhs; individual chapters, the contributors

The right of Jaimie Baron and Kristen Fuhs to be identified as the authors of the editorial material, and of the authors for their individual chapters, has been asserted in accordance with sections 77 and 78 of the Copyright, Designs and Patents Act 1988.

All rights reserved. No part of this book may be reprinted or reproduced or utilised in any form or by any electronic, mechanical, or other means, now known or hereafter invented, including photocopying and recording, or in any information storage or retrieval system, without permission in writing from the publishers.

Trademark notice: Product or corporate names may be trademarks or registered trademarks, and are used only for identification and explanation without intent to infringe.

ISBN: 978-1-032-50253-3 (hbk)
ISBN: 978-1-032-50254-0 (pbk)
ISBN: 978-1-003-39760-1 (ebk)

DOI: 10.4324/9781003397601

Typeset in Times New Roman
by Apex CoVantage, LLC

Contents

List of Figures   vii
Foreword   ix

Introduction: Constituting a Congregation in/through *Summer of Soul*   1
JAIMIE BARON

1   ***Summer of Soul*: The Angel of History Comes to Harlem**   6
CATHERINE RUSSELL

2   **The Black Archival Impulse**   21
LAUREN MCLEOD CRAMER

3   **Beyond Black Woodstock: *Summer of Soul* as Historical Recovery**   34
LANDON PALMER

4   **A Secret History of the Secret History of the 1969 Harlem Cultural Festival: *Summer of Soul*, The Staple Singers, and the Rockumentary Genre**   47
ANTHONY KINIK

5   **"Music in the Air": Spirituality and Revival in *Summer of Soul***   64
MICHELE PRETTYMAN

Bibliography   78
Contributor Bios   83
Index   85

Figures

1.1	Hal Tulchin's archive of video tapes, as pictured in *Summer of Soul*	7
1.2	An example of the video "noise" from the film's opening sequence	10
1.3	The Staple Singers onstage at the Harlem Cultural Festival singing "It's Been a Change"	13
1.4	Stevie Wonder singing in a close up, dissolving from a medium shot of him playing keys	17
2.1	Musa Jackson watches Hal Tulchin's footage of the Harlem Cultural Festival on an off-screen monitor during the documentary's opening sequence	23
2.2 and 2.3	Close up and long shot of Harlem Cultural Festival attendees during the documentary's opening sequence	27
2.4	Using an animated effect that resembles a grease pencil used to edit or annotate a contact sheet, *Summer of Soul* performs the repeated gestures of archival work, marking the film's reaction to archival material	29
3.1 and 3.2	Archival performance footage of The Edwin Hawkins Singers at the Harlem Cultural Festival is juxtaposed with other archival materials, exemplifying *Summer of Soul*'s approach to contextualization	40
4.1	The Staple Singers perform "Respect Yourself" in *Wattstax*	54
4.2	The Staple Singers perform "Help Me Jesus" in *Summer of Soul*	56
4.3	Mavis Staples and Mahalia Jackson perform "Precious Lord" in *Summer of Soul*	58
5.1	An image of Mavis Staples superimposed over the crowd emphasizes the ethereal oneness between performer and audience	73

Foreword

Docalogue began in 2017 – and continues – as an online journal, but it also began as a documentary salon in Los Angeles a decade earlier when the editors were both graduate students. Each month, we and a number of friends and colleagues would meet at one of our homes to watch and discuss a documentary film. Although the salon only lasted a year or so, it was one of the most stimulating forums for discussion of documentary film that we experienced during our graduate years. When the editors each moved on to academic jobs in different cities, we continued to meet at conferences, particularly Visible Evidence, which provides a major forum for documentary screening and discussion. Although Visible Evidence is always exciting and generative, we longed to have a way to sustain our discussions of documentary media throughout the year. From this desire arose Docalogue, a digital publication wherein we select one recent documentary each month and solicit two scholars to write a short essay about it, offering two perspectives intended to start off a broader conversation, whether on the website, in classrooms, or within documentary scholarship more broadly.

After about a year of provocative posts in this form, we decided that we might expand the Docalogue format to include short, edited books offering multiple perspectives on a single documentary film – a format that had rarely been tried, at least for nonfiction media. One of the challenges we have faced is how to decide which documentaries to choose as subjects of book-length study. On the website, this is less pressing since we feature so many documentaries, and the purpose is simply to foster scholarly conversation. In choosing documentaries for the book series, however, we are by definition singling out particular documentaries that we think have more than passing significance. And, since our focus is recent documentaries, this is necessarily a gamble: we do not know for certain which films will stand the test of time. In addition, while our aim is not to establish a new canon, by virtue of focusing a whole book on a film, we cannot help but raise the profile of the film at least within the documentary scholarly community. In the end, we decided to take the risk and simply choose films that we believe raise important issues about documentary in the contemporary moment and open themselves up to multiple avenues of scholarly analysis. Moreover, our aim is also to center at least some films that emerge from makers whose voices have not always been foregrounded by documentary scholarship.

The purpose of the Docalogue book series is, however, not to close the book, as it were, on any film. The idea is to open up conversation among scholars, to demonstrate to students the many ways of approaching a documentary text, and to offer a resource for those who wish to teach recent documentary films about which little has been written so far. We hope that, like the online journal, the book series will give rise to further scholarship about the films in question.

We would like to thank our Board of Advisors – Chris Cagle, Timothy Corrigan, Oliver Gaycken, Maria Pramaggiore, Pooja Rangan, Mila Turajlić, and Janet Walker – for their advice and suggestions regarding the selection of films and writers. Thanks to Natalie Foster, Sheni Kruger, and the whole team at Routledge for supporting this series. Our gratitude goes out to all of the writers who have contributed thus far to the Docalogue project – in both the book series and on the website.

For more information about the Docalogue, go to www.docalogue.com.

Introduction

Constituting a Congregation in/ through *Summer of Soul*

Jaimie Baron

Media are, in some sense, the root of all sociality. Human beings are gregarious, textual animals. Generally speaking, we like to be part of a group, a community, or at least an "imagined community," and we gather around texts of whatever medium. In times and places before or without written language, human beings gathered around storytellers and songs. After the invention of writing, communities formed around the repeated reading of particular religious or philosophical writings. More recently, communities – often communicating entirely through networked digital mediation – have formed around cult movies, video games, or Korean pop music.

Yet not all gatherings are the same. At times, we form congregations, a word that literally means to "come together" as a "herd" but whose connotations suggest a conscious choice, an intentional act of joining. Congregations, assemblies, and related collective configurations are engendered within social spaces where people gather to read (or otherwise experience) a text together, to listen to an exegesis on that text, to think and perhaps converse about what has been read or heard or said. Such a congregation can become the basis for reasoned action in the name of higher values: to redress, for instance, interpersonal grievances or unjust social inequities. At other times, we form mobs. The word "mob" comes from the same root as mobile or mobility. A mob is a group of people who "is moved" – affected from the outside, told what to think and what to do even if its members believe they are acting of their own volition. Frequently, the gathering of a mob results in violence against an "other" of some kind. The members of a congregation retain the power to question, to complicate, and to act collectively for the common good; the members of a mob relinquish the faculty of independent thought. Media have the potential to engender both congregations and mobs; in creating an audience, they – however briefly – produce an imagined community of one kind or the other.

Unlike spectators at sports matches or political rallies, for instance, audiences who gather around music require no opposition, no opponent, and concerts tend to be peaceful events.[1] In the case of musical performances, the act of congregation can become an occasion for shared joy, a celebration of simply being alive, here, now, together. Despite our many differences of

DOI: 10.4324/9781003397601-1

culture, class, politics, or opinion, human beings as a rule respond to music. It has been a central element of almost every religious practice (as well as most secular subcultures). Indeed, the fact that music festivals are not considered religious events may be testament to our overly limited definition of "religion." At a music festival, people gather to worship the beauty of organized sound, a particular arrangement of notes performed by a secular prophet – the musician – who creates sonic patterns capable of incurring an experience of collective ecstasy. Such ecstasy exceeds any particular creed. Asked about his religious affiliation, saxophonist Charlie Parker responded, "I am a devout musician."[2] Indeed, what we are watching and – nearly, vicariously, virtually – partaking of in director Ahmir "Questlove" Thompson's *Summer of Soul (. . .Or, When the Revolution Could Not Be Televised)* is no less than a religious event. This would be true even without the explicitly religious lyrics of many of the songs.

Watching *Summer of Soul* in a darkened cinema in July 2021, just as the pandemic was lifting and it felt *almost* safe to sit in a closed space with a group of strangers, I felt transported. Seeing the onscreen audience, its members' ghosts emerging from the recently discovered (or rediscovered) footage of the 1969 Harlem Cultural Festival, gathered in Mount Morris Park in the heat of summer to watch Stevie Wonder perform his sonic miracles, I felt like I, too, was standing in that crowd, cheering and dancing and celebrating *this moment* – despite and alongside tragedy. Although the musical sets that Questlove included in his film are much longer than those in most concert films, the duration felt like no chore. Although the Harlem Cultural Festival occurred before I was born and was staged for a local community to which I do not belong, I could feel the thrill of (almost) being in that audience, of the shared euphoria of the adoring crowd, a congregation gathered by and around music.

Of course, watching a retrospective documentary can never feel quite like attending the actual event. No film can replicate the sensation of clothes damp with humidity and sweat, the smells of street foods mixed with that of trampled grass, nor the sense of possible threat that came with gatherings at a time when the words "riot" and "assassination" appeared regularly in newspaper headlines. Yet, sound – and music, in particular – carries with it such potency that the recording is hardly less affectively powerful than the original sound. We viewers now cannot be fully copresent at the 1969 festival, but the music – suddenly (re)united with the performing bodies onstage – offers a sense of transtemporally joined perceptions, a shared experience of timbre, pitch, and beat. The recordings of the Harlem Cultural Festival – and their renewal in the form of a feature film – allow for the constitution of a much wider audience than the original ones could. Indeed, the fact that a dorky white Jewish woman like me can "attend" this concert at all speaks to the ways in which texts (musical, cinematic, and otherwise) can bring people together as audiences across vast chasms of time, space, and identity. The possibility of a broader, even transhistorical congregation comes, albeit briefly and phantasmatically, into being.

Cinema, like music, can bring people together, peacefully, without enemy or opponent.[3] As we shift toward streaming films at home, the imagined community that emerges in the form of a cinema audience becomes ever more virtual and (at least physically) disconnected. In the theater, I felt transported across cultural, geographical, and temporal boundaries, united across all those lines that divide. However, when I rewatched *Summer of Soul* at home, by myself, on my television screen, the sensation of being part of that crowd was dulled. Too aware of myself sitting in my apartment, distracted by the straggling strands of my daily life, the film was now about other people at another time. There were still moments when the music pulled me back in, but I no longer felt a part of the congregation.

Nevertheless, the historical promise of the film remains. These musical prophets were trying to point us toward a better future, and each of the five chapters in this volume explores how *Summer of Soul* opens onto wider issues of history, the archive, music, and genre. Catherine Russell's chapter "*Summer of Soul*: The Angel of History Comes to Harlem" takes up the question of time, revisiting Walter Benjamin's writings on history to explore how the past of 1969, the past-present of Questlove's 2021 production, and the present moment of viewing the film (shifting ever further into the future) collide and inform one another in *Summer of Soul*. Drawing on Kara Keeling's discussions of Black futures, Russell contends that the film opens a space for imagining what might have been and what still might be: an anti-racist future for all.

Lauren McLeod Cramer's chapter, "The Black Archival Impulse," expands on Hal Foster's notion of the "archival impulse" to articulate a specifically Black form of engagement with the archive or, alternatively, a different form of engagement with the archival traces of Black experience. Cramer reads *Summer of Soul* as an articulation of the ambivalence Black artists, and audiences often feel toward both the archiving and public display of Black history. On the one hand, the erasure or inaccessibility of Black history dispossesses contemporary Black people of their cultural history; on the other hand, the collection and display of artifacts of Black history always carry with them the threat of objectification and exploitation by others. Cramer reads *Summer of Soul* as positing collectivity as an alternative to collection. Both the collectivity displayed in images of the crowds gathered at Mount Morris Park and the collective acts of reception with the film by Questlove and others watching the "lost" footage together resist attempts to transform Black history into something "useable" by others.

Landon Palmer's chapter, "Beyond Black Woodstock: *Summer of Soul* as Historical Recovery," contextualizes *Summer of Soul* within the wider field of the popular music documentary, arguing that the "rockist" (i.e., white) tendencies of the genre and its historicization are countered here by the power of Black musical performance and Questlove's intervention. Indeed, although the Harlem Cultural Festival is now understood, in part, through comparison to Woodstock, Palmer argues that *Summer of Soul* demands that we rethink our narratives of 1960s musical practice and performance. Embedded in everyday (Black) urban space rather than situated "outside" of society and ordinary life, the Harlem Cultural Festival offers a different understanding of the experience and politics of musical performance and reception in American cultural life. In other words, rather than proposing an alternative to existing society, it demonstrates the ability of musical performance to transform everyday life.

Yet, *Summer of Soul* is by no means the first film about a Black music festival. Anthony Kinik brings Questlove's film into conversation with two other documentaries about festivals of Black music held soon after the Harlem Cultural Festival – *Soul to Soul* (Denis Sanders, 1971) and *Wattstax* (Mel Stuart, 1973). The Staple Singers appeared in all three of these films, and through close analysis of The Staple Singers' performance in each, Kinik explores their role in establishing and shaping the broader "rockumentary" genre and contextualizes their career and performances within the Black Arts Movement.

Finally, Michele Prettyman's chapter examines the Harlem Cultural Festival and *Summer of Soul* as extensions or instantiations of Black spirituality. Taking seriously the "soul" in *Summer of Soul*, she links the film to Black revivalism, a form of ecstatic collective catharsis aimed ultimately at positive personal and social transformation. In her analysis, she traces the many ways in which spirituality emerges in the film and identifies two styles of spiritual performance in the concert and film. The New Age style, exemplified by The 5th Dimension and Sly and the Family Stone, combined a Black spiritual ethos with a cosmic humanism, embracing both Black pride and universal humanity. Meanwhile, the gospel performances by The Staple Singers and Mahalia Jackson, rooted in Black history and spiritual practice, constitute a potentially transformative experience akin to a religious awakening.

Notably, had it not been for the "lostness" of the footage, Questlove's film might have simply been received as a well-made concert documentary rather than as a radical revision of multiple histories. There is little as compelling, however, as a "time capsule," which brings with it the sense of something appearing "suddenly" out of the past, innocent of the intervening years. Indeed, as artificial intelligence threatens to undermine indexical authority once and for all, the time capsule becomes even more precious, not only for its presumed authenticity but also for its related potential for historical insight. At a moment of continued social struggle around race, identity, and justice, the sudden reemergence of this footage – of a concert held just after the assassination of Rev. Dr. Martin Luther King Jr. that brought so much hope to an end – promises the possibility of a renewed historical consciousness, perhaps an alternative vision of what the present (our now) might have been and, hence, of a way of thinking a better (less racist, more peaceful) future together. Such lost footage found feels almost sacred, like a prophecy rediscovered. Yet prophecies are not promises. Can music and cinema help us form a congregation despite our differences and divisions? Or, feeding on self-righteousness and hatred of the other, will we succumb to the lure of the mob? *Summer of Soul* offers a vision of congregation onscreen as well as an invitation to the audiences today to join a wider congregation united – across time, space, and human difference – through the combined power of music and cinema.

Notes

1. There are, of course, exceptions, most famously including the 1969 Altamont Speedway Free Festival and Woodstock 99. More recently, angry fans have thrown cellphones at performers. See, for instance, *Gimme Shelter* (Albert and David Maysles, Charlotte Zwerin, 1970), *Woodstock 99: Peace, Love and Rage* (Garret Price, 2021), and Alaina Demopoulos, "From Bebe Rexha to Steve Lacy: Why Are Fans Throwing Phones at Musicians?," *The Guardian*, June 22, 2023. However, these incidents appear to be anomalous within the wider context of musical performance.
2. Lewis MacAdams, *Birth of the Cool: Beat, Bebop, and the American Avant Garde* (Simon & Schuster, 2012), 153.
3. There certainly have been instances of violence at movie screenings, but – as with musical performance – these are exceptions rather than the rule. See, for instance, Jason Bailey, "A Brief History of Violence in American Movie Theaters," *Flavorwire*, July 24, 2015.

1 *Summer of Soul*
The Angel of History Comes to Harlem

Catherine Russell

As an archive-based film, *Summer of Soul* is in many ways a perfect illustration of the significance of Walter Benjamin's claim that "In order for a part of the past to be touched by the present instant [*Aktualität*] there must be no continuity between them."[1] *Summer of Soul* is subtitled "When the revolution could not be televised," a line borrowed from Gil Scott-Heron, for whom it was a critique of the banality of white TV. The irony is, of course, that the Harlem Cultural Festival was televised in 1969, although its broadcast was limited to two one-hour segments at reputedly obscure hours with little to no publicity.[2] *Summer of Soul* is described in the film itself as made up of footage unseen until "now." In this chapter, I want to press a little harder on this now-time to see how this powerful concert film articulates revolutionary time through archival retrieval, digitization, and editing. The way that the film crystalizes the parallels between 1969 and 2021 in terms of Black Power, Black Lives Matter, and Black soul music produces a complex temporality that is at once utopian, mystical, and grounded in affective experience. It challenges the viewer to consider their own "now" as the precipice of a future that might echo the collective Harlem Cultural Festival experience of 1969.

For Walter Benjamin, "each 'now' is the now of a particular recognizability," and "the now of recognizability is the moment of awakening."[3] Does this film answer to such a recognizability? Can the original 1969 concert and its re-production 50 years later be seen and felt as a messianic moment of social change and transformation, an instance of the revolution that was and wasn't televised? If yes, it does so through a discourse of affect. The footage itself expresses the urgent conjunction of Black music and civil rights activism through performance and spectatorship. The editing of that footage as a mode of memory and the timing of the release of the film during the Covid-19 pandemic arguably produce a revolutionary dialectic of historical time, a dialectic of then and now that poses the question of: what next?

The framing of the *Summer of Soul* footage as having been lost, abandoned, and buried in a basement is an important part of its narrative. Because the festival had been "forgotten" by the culture at large, the finished film is a redemptive gesture. This is not recycled footage, although many of the

DOI: 10.4324/9781003397601-2

contextual archival clips and photos have been retrieved and recycled from institutional archives and are therefore instances of archival media research, appropriated and reused. Director Ahmir "Questlove" Thompson and his editor Joshua L. Pearson have also included newly shot interviews with festival participants looking back at the concert footage "watching their younger selves" and remembering their experience.[4] For Benjamin, "while the relation of the present to the past is purely temporal, the relation of what-has-been to the now is dialectical; not temporal in nature but figural."[5] Through the nonlinear editing of these multiple time frames, *Summer of Soul* produces a dialectical historiography of American culture.

It is precisely because *Summer of Soul* is composed from archival images (the figural) that Benjamin's messianic historiography is so appropriate. Moreover, the extent to which the film is constructed from sound as well as image archives makes it further exemplary of the Black futurist discourse produced by filmmaker John Akomfrah and Black studies scholar Kara Keeling, both of whom are informed by Benjamin's historiography. My approach to the film, highlighting the commonalities between these thinkers, situates the popular documentary as a virtual incarnation of Benjamin's Angel of History. The future that the Angel foresees cannot be imagined without technology, spiritual faith, sensory experience, and the fragmented temporality of archival re-use. This is a future that has yet to arrive, but its seeds are in the debris and the struggle of the past. Both Akomfrah and Keeling build on Benjamin's historiography to imagine the role of music and/as technology as the crucible of thinking through the catastrophe of now-time and to clear space for a different kind of future.

Figure 1.1 Hal Tulchin's archive of video tapes, as pictured in *Summer of Soul*.

The time of the pandemic, which allowed Questlove the time to sort through the footage, was also the historical moment when the reckless murder of George Floyd and the vivid evidence of systemic racial discrimination during the Trump era spurred on the urgency of the Black Lives Matter movement.[6] That now-time is brought together with the time of the 1969 festival, and the time of viewing *Summer of Soul*, which links five different concert days and uses many superimpositions in which the multiple angles of five video cameras are combined into one musical, rhythmic time.[7] Walter Benjamin's admonition to "appropriate a memory as it flashes up in a moment of danger" rests on the observation that "articulating the past historically does not mean recognizing it 'the way it really was'." The historian needs to fan "the spark of hope in the past" by tearing it apart.[8] In my book, *Archiveology*, I argue that this destructive gesture is a critical tool of archival film practices through which new histories are made from the ruined image cultures of the past.[9] As Keeling has noted, film is uniquely suited to this task, and if Isaac Julien's *Looking for Langston* (1989) performed such a task for the Harlem Renaissance, then *Summer of Soul* performs a similar action for Harlem of the 1960s.[10] In "tearing apart" and reconstituting the footage of the Harlem Culture Festival, *Summer of Soul* opens a space for thinking about potential futures – particularly Black futures but also futures shared across culture and identity – both then (1969) and when the film was made (2021) and into the ongoing present.

Keeling's notion of Black futures, like Heron's conception of the untelevised revolution, is theorized by and for African Americans and people of color globally. Working through "Bartleby," a short story by Herman Melville, in which an accountant tells his boss that he "would prefer not to" do his job, Keeling cites Giorgio Agamben suggesting that Bartleby "keeps possibility suspended between occurrence and non-occurrence, between capacity to be and capacity not to be." To put this in other terms, Bartleby for Keeling is a figure of "futures past."[11] Keeling's method resembles Benjamin's in her stacking of quotations – including some from Benjamin himself – for a theory akin to Benjamin's dialectical images.

Keeling's theorization of Black futures is grounded in the material histories of Black existence, but she also notes that "the long arc of Black existence contains vital elements that might be recombined to call forth new relations for all."[12] I would further clarify this notion of Black futures as belonging to everyone who would prefer to live in an anti-racist world in which racial equality is normalized. As Keeling notes, Black existence "carries within it alternative organizations of time in which the future, if there is such a thing, has not been promised; it has had to be created by reaching through and beyond what exists."[13] Growing up with soul music as many white women of my generation did, without understanding its roots in a violent colonial history, *Summer of Soul* is for me a mode of enlightenment and social justice through which I can remake my own memory, to imagine a different Black anti-racist future for everyone. Indeed, one of the key accomplishments of the revisiting of the Harlem Cultural Festival of 1969 is that its memory of possibility held in suspension is made available beyond the original Harlem audience to viewers of all ages and races. The address of the original event may have been specifically to the Harlem community, but in 2021 the concert film was broadcast internationally, addressing millions of potential new allies of the Black struggle.

What Time Is It Now?

The opening sequence of *Summer of Soul* poses the question of when is "now" very specifically. Concert attendee Musa Jackson, one of many who the producers identified through social media,[14] is shot in close-up with a blank face. An off-screen voice asks him if he remembers the Harlem Cultural Festival, and his face brightens with the blue light of the monitor, although his expression remains hesitant and uncertain. Cut to a festival audience in unsteady, unfocused camera movements (a note of uncertainty never to be repeated in the film). Many of the cuts in the opening sequence are marked by a flash of video "noise." A loudspeaker announces a lost wallet – implicitly also announcing a non-violent crime-free space – before intertitles state the time and place of the concert "100 miles from Woodstock," and then "It has never been seen. Until now." Cut to the crowd under umbrellas. Concert promoter Tony Lawrence briefly introduces Stevie Wonder, who launches into "It's Your Thing," while the camera picks out individual dancers in the crowd: a young boy and a woman in pink. Wonder moves to the drum kit for "Drum Solo" while the montage moves through flash forwards to forthcoming acts, all of them dancing, synched to Wonder's drum solo, which is shot from multiple camera angles, superimposed over one another in a frenzy of musical energy. The sound of the band is lowered, and we hear fragments of dialogue, including someone declaiming on a dark stage, "What time is it?" followed by voice-over clips describing the transformational moment of the summer of 1969. "We were creating a new world," one man says, and another voice describes the summer as a "Black Consciousness Revolution."

What time is "now"? It could be when Musa Jackson first sees the footage (and if that was really when and where the film says it was), or when someone wrote the intertitle "until now," or when the director and producers first saw the footage, or when someone watches the film today, whenever that is. The opacity created around the timing of "now" foregrounds the present-tense and its transience. Precisely because now-time is rendered so fleeting, the possibility of social change is, in Benjamin's words, "blasted out of the continuum."[15] The now-time of the Harlem Cultural Festival 1969 is, in part, a mythic time when violence and crime were temporarily banished, when the city park was a space of collective love, Black Power, and family. But *Summer of Soul* does not deny or repress the underlying tensions of violence and anti-Black racism.

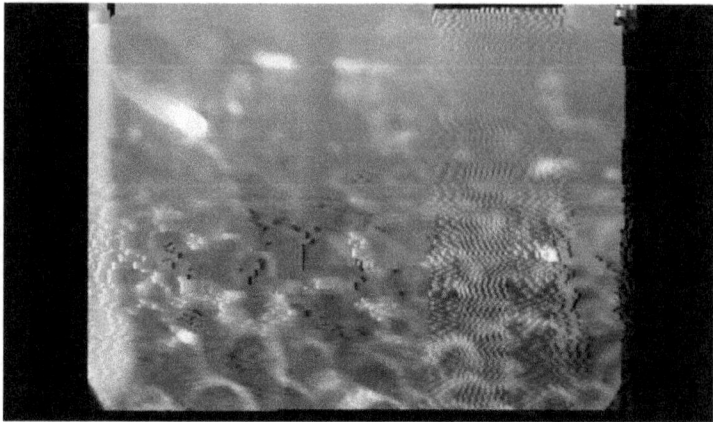

Figure 1.2 An example of the video "noise" from the film's opening sequence.

The violence of Harlem in 1968, when Black Americans brought New York to its knees after the assassination of Martin Luther King Jr. is only briefly alluded to in the film. The aftermath and ongoing cultural landscape of drug use, poverty, and ruination are, however, palpable. The brightly decorated stage of the festival and the sunshine and visceral energy of the audience dancing, clapping, and pulsing cannot erase its haunting presence. Political speeches by Jesse Jackson, who channels King, and mayor John Lindsay, the "blue-eyed soul brother" who thanks and flatters the Harlem community, thinly mask the violence lying behind the celebration of Black culture. Mavis Staples and Mahalia Jackson singing "My Precious Lord," however, most powerfully and persuasively transform the crippling pain of King's passing into a call for collective action. Mahalia passing the mic to Mavis is an act of generational transition and renewal, felt not only by Staples herself but by the audience of the concert and the audience of the film.

Much is made in the film and about the film regarding the heterogeneity of the Black music featured in *Summer of Soul*. Blues, jazz, gospel, salsa, and soul music are brought together as one Black musical form grounded in rhythm. The pulse is apparent not only on the stage but in the audience, whose dancing bodies are picked out by Hal Tulchin's five video cameras. In fact, this singular music is probably best described as soul, which Emily J. Lordi defines as possessing a "recuperative logic" and an "alchemy of pain."[16] Soul emerged as a popular term precisely during the 1960s as a mode of social organization and an "open-ended readiness" for a people in transition.[17] The term was popularized at a time of crisis to define resiliency and "thriving," but the promised "transition," along with the promised revolution, has yet to happen. In 2021, *Summer of Soul* poses the critical question of the potential of

Summer of Soul 11

soul music to inspire real social change and a truly anti-racist public sphere. What happened to the revolution that was and wasn't televised that summer in Marcus Garvey Park (or Mount Morris Park as it was then called)? The future that was imagined in 1969 is "now" – the present – but as Lordi puts it at the end of her book *The Meaning of Soul*, "If we are the future that past artists and activists dreamed of, how much freer were we all supposed to be?"[18] Keeling's theory of Black futures builds on the Afrofuturist aesthetics that were roughly concurrent with the Harlem Cultural Festival, but in an avant-garde modality. The Afro-futurism of Sun Ra offered a futurist discourse for the sense of crisis, urgency, and community for African Americans, through the recognition of African heritage alongside the rejection of American racist institutions. Afrofuturism was a free jazz movement that embraced new technologies of the 1960s, including space travel, and the cameras and TV set-up that made *Summer of Soul* possible. Keeling is critical of the proto-colonial impulse of Sun-Ra's film *Space Is the Place* (1974), where a Black future transpires on another planet. In the Afrofuturist narrative, for Keeling, "a Black future is no future at all."[19] At the same time, because it is grounded in free jazz and poetry, Afrofuturism points to "a way to enter into relation with an autochthonous space of and for Black existence. Such a world is not premised on dispossession, ownership, property, and exploitation."[20] The same can be said of the Harlem Cultural Festival and its reconstruction in 2021, where the history of inner-city poverty and violence is inverted and reframed as a love-in. Keeling's futurism recognizes the significance of "Black Swan" events, or surprising eruptions that are at once unpredictable and yet have a high impact.[21] Is this not a good description of the Harlem Cultural Festival, especially in its belated recycled form, as an awakening after 50 years of dormancy?

The festival, as reconstructed by Questlove and his team, seems to have created a utopian space of Black experience, and yet neither the film nor the festival can be said to be free of the logic of consumer capitalism, as Keeling imagines Black futurism to be. The festival was sponsored by Maxwell House coffee, even if it also received support from the city of New York; the documentary was co-produced by Disney and released in the United States on the streaming platform Hulu, which counts Disney as its majority stakeholder. The celebrity musicians who performed at the festival are embedded in the industrial complex of popular culture and were hopefully compensated by the sponsors then and now. While Keeling's futurism leans toward the avant-garde, the soul music performed on the Harlem stage – including its multiple subcategories of jazz, blues, and gospel – is consumed by families alongside hipsters. Unlike Afrofuturism, which was addressed to specialized audiences of the avant-garde, *Summer of Soul* is eminently consumable.

While it is no surprise that Thompson and his producers chose to make a movie with broad appeal from the spectacular footage, it does raise the question of its revolutionary value. After all, Heron's poem from which the subtitle is borrowed proposes that the revolution will take place on the street, not on the screen. And yet, in its articulation of now-time and its crystallization of present and past, a present-tense of renewed Black activism, *Summer of Soul* may in fact construct an Afrofuturism for the 21st century, appropriating the affective energy of 1969 for a renewal of the promise of soul. Heron's poem includes the line, "The revolution will put you in the driver's seat," and the film arguably does this by addressing the spectator as a participant in the "new world" created in retrospect by the 1969 Festival.

Archival Montage as Digitopia

Walter Benjamin's Angel of History predicates the impossible future on the chaos of the past: "Where a chain of events appears before *us, he* sees one single catastrophe, which keeps piling wreckage upon wreckage and hurls it at his feet."[22] Keeling, building on Benjamin's historiography and Sun Ra's declaration "It's after the end of the world. Don't you know that yet?" belted out by June Tyson in *Space Is the Place*, defines a Black future as having "another temporality and coordinates" that are neither predictable nor coherent.[23] In the temporal dissonance of past, present, and future, no continuity or stability presages a Black future. The aesthetics of montage and the art of archiveology, remaking history from recorded sounds and images, are vital tools for this project.[24] For Benjamin and Keeling, it is critical that the past is rendered sensual and affective, as a mode of experience. Sun Ra and Tyson's refrain "opens a marvellous (im)possibility: 'the world' does not cohere as such."[25]

Keeling also engages with *The Last Angel of History* (John Akomfrah, 1996), a film inspired by Benjamin's "Theses on the Philosophy of History," where Paul Klee's painting *Angelus Novus* is described as an Angel being blown into the future by the destructive storm of progress.[26] In this film, produced by Black Audio Film Collective, the "data thief" is an archiveologist, time-traveling to the sounds of Black music of the 1980s and 1990s, inspired by Sun-Ra's free jazz and speculative historiography. The data thief is impersonated by Blues guitarist Robert Johnson, and also by Parliament Funkadelic, while Akomfrah's collage style is pitched as a celebration of the emerging digital field. Indeed, Akomfrah has written about the digitopia of Black futures premised on the digital, which, for him, brings moving images closer to the rhythmic foundations of Black music and Black culture. While the Harlem Cultural Festival did include some free jazz according to Questlove, which the audience was surprisingly patient with, Sly and the Family Stone are the most funky and "psychedelic" of the lineup in the film.[27] The electronic and proto-digital instrumentation and aesthetics of Afrofuturism are clearly registered in the video glitch that marks the initial cuts of the film, inscribing the technologies at work in the art and act of resurrection.

Figure 1.3 The Staple Singers onstage at the Harlem Cultural Festival singing "It's Been a Change."

Both *Summer of Soul* and *The Last Angel of History* make reference to the moon landing of 1969, but the technological achievement has very different meanings in the two films. For Akomfrah, the moon landing represents a technological utopia, inspiring the interplanetary adventures of Sun Ra and Afrofuturism, while for Questlove and the Harlem Cultural Festival attendees, it is much less. In Akomfrah's film, Black astronaut Bernard Harris and Michelle Nichols, a diversity recruiter for NASA, talk about what it means for Black people to be included in the space program. Their accomplishments are unironically tied to George Clinton's "mothership connection" and the data thief's pronouncement that there is a profound connection between music, space, and the future. In *Summer of Soul*, as The Staple Singers sing "It's Been a Change," which includes the phrase "one of these days they'll be a man on the moon," Thompson intercuts interviews borrowed from TV news of the period in which the white interviewees praise the moon landing for its accomplishment for science, global harmony, and human achievement, but the Black interviewees disdain the event as a waste of money that could have been better spent helping poor Black people in America. One of the last interviewees segues the film into a sequence on the heroin epidemic in 1969 Harlem, and thus the film outright rejects any allegorical significance of outer space as an answer to the struggle for a better Black future. At the same time, by highlighting the racial divide of 1969, *Summer of Soul* foregrounds the rift between Black and White social imaginaries. An anti-racist future is one in which our goals are better aligned.

The moon-landing sequence is remarkable for the cutting back-and-forth between the singers and the sound bites. The Staples' song is about social change through hard work and education, addressed to the young people in the audience. The pulse of the song, a tight fusion of blues and gospel harmonies, is taken up by the editing, moving through the news footage, dancing audience members, and the three Staples sisters in medium close-up with matching dresses and afros. They are in synch with the audience, both ideologically and musically, challenging the dominant white narrative of the moon landing. The sequence includes Black anchormen wearing dashikis explaining the unpopularity of the moon landing for the Black community, a visual signature of an alternate televisual reality of the times. As one Black man-on-the-street puts it: "It's groovy for certain people but not for the Black man in America." Another says, "Black man wants to go to Africa; white man's going to the moon. I'm going to stay in Harlem with the Puerto Ricans and have me some fun."

In *The Last Angel of History*, the narrator declares that "Our thief from the future gives up the right to belong in his time in order to come to our time to find the mothership connection." Thompson is not a thief but a borrower, but his technique nevertheless invokes the mothership connection. For Emma Cocker, "borrowing" is the best term for artists' film and video works that re-use archival materials because it invokes the dialogue that takes place between present and past, a process of "meaning making," rather than a "retrieval of meaning from the past."[28] The recovery of the Harlem Cultural Festival is also a remaking of it, not only in the choice made to exclude some material, but in the cutting up of the show and mixing it with visual and audio evidence of the cultural history to which it was a response.

In the film, the songs are rebuilt, often through the use of dissolves, fluidly linked through clever sound edits that cover the cuts with rhythmic continuity. *Summer of Soul* is proof of Akomfrah's faith in the potential of digital tools as the answer to Black cinema grounded in the pulse of African-originated drumming.[29] For Akomfrah, the difference between analog and digital editing is the "fear of phantoms and loss" in analog editing when cut-out images are either gone completely or re-inserted with splice marks. He compares this to "digital editing with all its rhythmic possibilities, its banishing of the warrior mark by turning all images into ghosts, facsimiles without referent, all ghost and all machine."[30] Editor Joshua Pearson shares Questlove's background in VJ culture, and their approach to the archival material was that of the VJ rather than the experimental "found footage" filmmaker, which is where Akomfrah comes from. Akomfrah's embrace of the digital as the future of Black music lies in his recognition of the role of music in Black histories.[31] By digitizing the original analog tapes, Questlove and Pearson had more "rhythmic possibilities" for their edit, and yet both modes are *technologies* that enable the cut-up and fragmentation of archiveological method. Medium specificity is less important than the mechanics of editing together fragments of the past shared by analog and digital media.

Keeling follows Akomfrah's data thief's proclamation that the Blues is a secret Black technology to suggest that "a formulation of race as technology offers a way to conceptualize the possibilities for materialist anti-racist praxis that still inhere in the cinematic."[32] For both Keeling and Akomfrah, "the digital" is inherently atemporal, untethered from the space-time continuum of referentiality. Keeling develops Akomfrah's concept of digitopia as an "unmooring of spatiotemporal logics . . . including the proposition of wrenching the index from its referent."[33] In *Archiveology*, I make a similar argument about digital images as files having an immateriality that obliterates the discontinuity between images and reality in the sense that images are themselves "things" in the real world – as exemplified by the moving images that are the remnants of the Harlem Cultural Festival.[34] Joshua Pearson says that the tapes that were recovered in Tulchin's basement included no isolated camera reels, only live line cuts in which the various camera angles were already assembled and cut up, so he was essentially working with the bones of a concert film, not the concert itself.[35]

The digital distinctions between inside and outside collapse, which opens up the possibility of digitopian discourse of the African diaspora in the modality of Black music. The archival language of recycled sound and image enables new temporalities, new histories, and new futures: new "now-times." Keeling says that the data thief "structures a messianic time" through which cinematic technologies are responsible for another organization of things, "outside the tyranny of time." The digital realm as an immaterial space-time makes possible the meeting of past and future in an imaginary new memory-vision, especially when it is grounded in the affective, sensory rhythms of African American culture.

Because the Harlem Cultural Festival took place over several weekends in 1969, Tulchin's video footage includes performances and audiences from many different days, which are compounded into one long festival by Thompson and Pearson. The disjunctions between different concert days are nevertheless made evident by abrupt costume changes by recurring figures such as Tony Lawrence and Jesse Jackson, and by the variety of weather conditions, from extreme heat to pouring rain. In this sense, *Summer of Soul* echoes *Amazing Grace* (Alan Elliott, 2018), made from footage shot by Sydney Pollack, another archival reconstruction that combines two of Aretha Franklin's 1972 concerts in a Los Angeles Baptist church into one moving and spectacular movie. Aretha seems to change her outfit in the middle of songs, as the editors reconstructed her performance from multiple sound recordings and camera angles collected over two different nights. In both cases, the status of the films as digital constructions is foregrounded as disjunctive temporalities synched through rhythm and soul music. Both films push their archival status to the foreground, situating the powerful musical performances outside of linear time, creating new composite and nonlinear times that open the possibility of imagining different pasts and futures.

The dynamic technologies and the wide-ranging content of *Summer of Soul* arguably bring it close to the digitopia conceived by Akomfrah and the impossible future imagined by Keeling on several levels. First of all, the diasporic reach of the film is grounded in the back-to-Africa ethos of the 1960s, including the brightly colored fashions, the participation of Hugh Masakela and the Dinizulu Dancers and Drummers, and is inclusive of Latin music in the form of Puerto Rican drummer and bandleader Ray Barretto. Second, a strong digitopian thrust of *Summer of Soul* lies in the transposition of analog video to digital code, enabling the multilayered and synched editing of images and sounds. And finally, the "messianic" historiography is felt most strongly in the shared experience of 21st-century viewers of all races in our own time, mostly in our own homes, and the thriving throng of Black bodies in 1969, dancing to the same music. By stressing the deep links between gospel and soul, the reconstructed Harlem Cultural Festival embraces the spiritual roots of Black music, implicitly inscribing the redemptive impulse of Benjamin's historiography.

The Future Anterior

The final scenes of *Summer of Soul* drive home the urgency of the revival of the 1960s alliance of activism and soul music in 2021. Nina Simone concludes her performance with the recitation of a poem backed by a chant: "Are you ready?" She asks the audience if they are ready to kill if necessary, or to smash and burn buildings. A news clip from the period features Black protesters and white police arguing in Harlem, while the repeated phrase "are you ready?" continues. Simone's invocation of violence jumps out of the peaceful celebration of Black community and is the film's only hint at divisions within the Black activism of the times, between peaceful and violent protest. As Daphne Brooks has noted, Simone was deeply informed by Brechtian aesthetics in which her performance was often a mode of activism and agitation.[36]

Simone's set is followed by a brief blackout, before black-and-white photos show the deserted park, littered with the evidence of a vanished crowd. The jarring shift from Simone's vibrant African print dress and stunning hairdo to the banality of urban waste is echoed by a voice remarking on the colorful beauty of the forgotten concerts. Stacks of videotapes denote the archive that Tulchin says, in voice-over, he could not sell to anyone. Shots of the crowd in black and white reinforce the aesthetic of erasure and neglect, while a woman's voice speaks of the importance of the Festival "especially today," when Black people need to feel "like a family." Cut to a final performance of Sly and the Family Stone singing "Higher," with the audience singing along and Rose Stone gyrating with her white wig and silver dress.

The reference to family is apt but undersells the film's gift of energy and high-powered, high-level musicianship. Stevie Wonder's extended performance toward the end of the film is a good example of how Thompson and Pearson's editing of the archival footage expands its affect. Even though it is interrupted by a brief bio of Wonder explaining how he became a Civil Rights activist around the time of the Festival, the footage of him playing keyboards

Figure 1.4 Stevie Wonder singing in a close up, dissolving from a medium shot of him playing keys.

and singing is especially rich and dynamic. Shots of his feet rhythmically stomping and working the keyboard pedal are superimposed over shots of him singing, looking skyward, standing, and bouncing until his bandleader gently coaxes him into ending the runaway song. Digital effects are used here to layer the images into a palimpsest of explosive energy. The urgency of Wonder's spirit is as palpable as Simone's polemics, or Jesse Jackson's rhetoric, and is what makes the film turn toward a future grounded in a past experience of shared struggle.

The story of the "lost" tapes is also a story of how American cultural history has been written. The working title of "Black Woodstock" certified the Festival's status as a shadow of the other event. And yet, it is precisely because Hal Tulchin not only taped the Festival so well, providing multiple camera angles of the performances as well as extensive footage of the faces and bodies and dance steps of the audience, but safeguarded the material too, that the film was made possible. For all its digitopian promise, *Summer of Soul* remains a record, on one level, of what really happened. To say that the film is a new thing, made in a new "now" does not contradict its status as evidentiary. The relation between past and future inscribed in this film may be described as a "coil," a fold, or a discontinuous memory that originates from the future. Domietta Torlasco describes the "future anterior" as "one that remembers not only what happened but also what did not happen in our cinematic past."[37]

Thompson's film not only rewrites American cultural history; it also enables a re-imagining of the potential of a different future. As Keeling proposes, such a future "can be conceptualized as a creative, eccentric way of sinking deeply into the space held open in music and engaging with what is always there already."³⁸ Benjamin's Angel of History sees a messianic future constructed from the failures of the past – from the chaos, violence, and barbarism of the past, but also from the unfulfilled promises that failure inaugurates. Thus, the revolutionary discourse embedded in the soul manifesto becomes "legible" in 2021 during the anti-racist activism generated by police brutality made newly visible through digital means and the large-scale protests under the banner of Black Lives Matter.

The pandemic context meant that the image of Black crowds packed into a joyful time, at a moment when even street protests required social distancing, had extra impact. The crowd of mostly male bodies waiting for Sly and the Family Stone to take the stage seems to sway like an ocean, as if it were one large Black body. The "now" of the film, half a century later, includes the time when that image becomes legible as a force of power and collective energy. A loudspeaker threatens the crowd to be patient as the seething sea of bodies harbors seeds of revolt, marking roads not taken.

Summer of Soul points to a "future anterior" of a Black future grounded in past sensory experience. For Torlasco, the "future anterior" refers to "what will have been." It "embodies the promises of temporal excess and becoming, providing feminist theory with the possibility of envisioning a future that does not resemble the past."³⁹ In Benjamin's theory of history, montage and ruins play significant roles, as the "refuse" of history is precisely where the future lies. Tulchin's tapes may never have been considered "garbage" – except for those who refused to buy them or broadcast them – but their "lostness" has everything to do with their previous devaluation and their contrasting power in the present. Benjamin's "awakening" is premised on the claim that "'Historical understanding' is to be grasped, in principle, as the afterlife of that which is understood."⁴⁰

Questlove's project challenges the audience to ask what happened to that revolutionary energy of summer 1969, and yet "the present" is forever being eclipsed by another "now-time," and it is precisely that other "now-time" of 2021 that makes *Summer of Soul* exemplary of Benjamin's Angel of History. He notes in *The Arcades Project* that the "historical index" of images only becomes legible at a particular time, and this "acceding to legibility constitutes a specific critical point in the movement at their interior."⁴¹ Can this be the movement of the people dancing at the Harlem Cultural Festival in 1969? The movement of the Pips choreography? Ray Baretta's drums, or the 5th Dimension exposing their gospel roots? Stevie Wonder levitating? Are they signaling a more equitable anti-racist America, or is it just my imagination?

Notes

1. Walter Benjamin, *The Arcades Project*, trans. Howard Eiland and Kevin McLaughlin (Cambridge, MA: Harvard University Press, 1999), 470.
2. According to the Wikipedia entry for the Harlem Cultural Festival, a one-hour special was broadcast by CBS on July 28, 1969, and a second one-hour was broadcast by *ABC* on September 16, 1969 (accessed February 16, 2023). Citation: James

Gaunt, "Who Is Tony Lawrence?" *The Shadow Knows*, December 21, 2001. These were said to be the first shows with commercials featuring all Black performers.
3. Benjamin, *The Arcades Project*, 463, 470.
4. Clifford Thompson, "'When Black Was Born': *Summer of Soul*," *Commonweal* 148, no. 8 (September 2021).
5. Benjamin, *The Arcades Project*, 463.
6. Questlove interviewed on *The Director's Cut*, November 1, 2021, https://podcasts.apple.com/ca/podcast/summer-of-soul-with-ahmir-questlove-thompson-and-amir/id1067471691?i=1000540450448.
7. Richard Sandomir, "Hal Tulchin, Who Documented a 'Black Woodstock,' Dies at 90," *New York Times*, September 14, 2017.
8. Walter Benjamin, "On the Concept of History," in *Selected Writings, Vol. 4 1938–40*, ed. Michael W. Jennings (Cambridge, MA: Harvard University Press, 2003), 390–91.
9. Catherine Russell, *Archiveology: Walter Benjamin and Archival Film Practices* (Durham, NC: Duke University Press, 2018).
10. Kara Keeling, *Queer Times, Black Futures. Sexual Cultures* (New York: New York University Press, 2020), 91.
11. Keeling, *Queer Times, Black Futures*, 48. Keeling quotes the phrase "futures past" from a book of the same name by David Scott (Duke University Press, 2004). Scott's opening words of that book are: "My most general concern in this book is with the conceptual problem of political presents and with how reconstructed pasts and anticipated futures are though out in relation to them." (1).
12. Keeling, *Queer Times, Black Futures*, 35.
13. Ibid.
14. *The Director's Cut*, podcast November 1, 2021.
15. Benjamin, *The Arcades Project*, 475.
16. Emily J. Lordi, *The Meaning of Soul: Black Music and Resilience Since the 1960s* (Durham, NC: Duke University Press, 2020), 8.
17. Lordi, *The Meaning of Soul*, 10.
18. Ibid., 163.
19. Keeling, *Queer Times, Black Futures*, 67.
20. Ibid., 69.
21. Ibid., 20. Keeling borrows the concept of the Black Swan from Nassim Nicholas Taleb, *The Black Swan: The Impact of the Highly Improbable* (New York: Random House Trade Paperbacks, 2010).
22. Benjamin, "On the Concept of History," 392.
23. Keeling, *Queer Times, Black Futures*, 53.
24. "Archiveology" is a term developed in my book *Archiveology: Walter Benjamin and Archival Film Practices* (Durham, NC: Durham University Press, 2018) to refer to media practices that engage with archival sounds and images through remediation and recycling. As a mode of found footage filmmaking, archiveology explicitly refers to the remaking and reconstructing of historical materials through archival retrieval.
25. Keeling, *Queer Times, Black Futures*, 54.
26. Edward George, who researched, wrote, and performed in *The Last Angel of History*, explains the integral role of Walter Benjamin in the conceptualization of the film and as inspiration for the title in "Last Angel of History: Research, Writing, Performance," *Third Text* 35 (2021): 205–26. He refers to the key essay as "Theses on the Philosophy of History," whereas I have cited the more recent translation as "On the Concept of History."
27. Questlove interviewed on *Object of Sound*, podcast July 9, 2021, https://object-of-sound.simplecast.com/episodes/summer-of-soul-feat-questlove.
28. Emma Cocker, "Ethical Possession: Borrowing from the Archives," in *Cultural Borrowings: Appropriation, Reworking, Transformation*, Scope 16 (February 2010), 102.

29. John Akomfrah, "Digitopia and the Spectres of Diaspora," *Journal of Media Practice* 11, no. 1 (January 2014): 26.
30. Akomfrah, "Digitopia and the Spectres of Diaspora," 26.
31. Joshua Pearson interviewed on Gold Derby, November 18, 2021, accessed February 18, 2023, www.youtube.com/watch?v=QviTLovSebo.
32. Keeling, *Queer Times, Black Futures*, 135.
33. Ibid., 137.
34. Russell, *Archiveology*, 103.
35. Joshua Pearson interviewed on Gold Derby.
36. Daphne A. Brooks, "Nina Simone's Triple Play," *Callaloo* 34, no. 1 (Winter 2011): 176–97.
37. Domietta Torlasco, *The Heretical Archive* (Minneapolis: Minnesota University Press, 2013), vi.
38. Keeling, *Queer Times, Black Futures*, 69.
39. Torlasco, *The Heretical Archive*, vii.
40. Benjamin, *The Arcades Project*, 460.
41. Ibid., 462.

2 The Black Archival Impulse

Lauren McLeod Cramer

The opening credit sequence of Ahmir "Questlove" Thompson's documentary *Summer of Soul (. . . Or, When the Revolution Could Not Be Televised)* (2021) includes images of an expectant crowd gathered outside on a sunny day, seemingly waiting for history to be made. The slightly warped footage scans a sizeable crowd that extends beyond the shaky edges of the frame, accompanied by a voice-over that explains, "Nobody ever heard of the Harlem Cultural Festival; nobody would believe it happened."[1] Before there is much time to consider the contradicting sound and image tracks, the film introduces its central conceit, a disclosure that promises to explain the incongruity of an 'unknown' event attended by thousands of people. In white text on a black screen, four intertitles state:

> In 1969, during the same summer as Woodstock, a different music festival took place 100 miles away. Over 300,000 people attended the summer concert series known as the Harlem Cultural Festival. It was free to all. The festival was filmed. But after that summer, the footage sat in a basement for 50 years. It has never been seen.

After a brief pause, the final statement is revised by the addition of two words, "Until now."

Summer of Soul, which is about the cinematic legacy of the 1969 Harlem Cultural Festival, begins by declaring itself as an event. The documentary, which was released simultaneously in theaters and online, recalls a sense of occasion formerly reserved for live performances or 'first-run' films.[2] While the premise – that the film accomplishes and is itself a historic achievement – is enticing, the press surrounding the film's release and its Academy Award win for Best Documentary Feature offers a slightly less remarkable account of the festival footage's provenance and its journey to big and small screens. For instance, parts of the video filmed by television director Hal Tulchin had been seen. Some performances from the festival aired on CBS in 1969 and overseas in the 1970s, and Tulchin and his collaborators had come close to making a documentary about the festival in the early 2000s. Additionally, in the time between that unrealized project and *Summer of Soul*, portions of the

DOI: 10.4324/9781003397601-3

footage appeared in other music documentaries.³ As *Summer of Soul* continues, it becomes increasingly clear that Questlove's film is, to great acclaim, recalling an event that already had virtually every condition for historic preservation and recognition in place. Thousands of people witnessed the festival; the festival was recorded; that record was properly preserved; and access to that record, while lacking publicity, was available. Of course, these facts only contribute to the sense of shock we might feel upon discovering that we have *not* already seen this star-studded footage of awe-inspiring Black musical performance. By perhaps overstating its historic contribution, *Summer of Soul* reserves a distinct space for art and occasions that feel singular, regardless of the actual precedent; ultimately, it reveals its involvement in this archival project is about affect more than accuracy. Questlove's film and the publicity surrounding it frame the concert series as familiar and unfamiliar, hidden and unhidden; and as a result, together, they articulate a feeling that is akin to the anxious anticipation of waiting for a live concert; the instant just "before the curtain goes up in the theater" and "the three taps of the conductor's baton" – these are the signals that the moment we've been waiting for is *already* here.⁴

On screen, that hopeful excitement is most clearly portrayed in the interview with Musa Jackson that bookends the film. Jackson, a Black man who attended the festival as a child, is introduced just after a shot of a film slate marking the still-untitled "Black Woodstock Doc" and the sound of crew members preparing to film. Once the set is clear, we see Jackson and hear Questlove ask from offscreen, "So, do you remember the Harlem Cultural Festival?" At that moment, archival footage begins to play on a monitor just beyond the frame, but the camera remains fixed on Jackson's stunned expression, slightly illuminated by the light of the screen. In its conclusion, *Summer of Soul* returns to Jackson, whose eyes are still reflecting the glowing screen as he nods, chokes back tears, and says, "Yeah." Jackson, volunteering a deeply personal explanation, says, "you put memories away, and you don't realize . . . sometimes you don't even know if they're real. So, it's almost confirmation that what I knew is real." From behind the camera the filmmaker responds, "Yeah, so you know you're not crazy." Jackson is overjoyed. He is so excited that he begins moving in and out of the camera's focus and unintentionally interrupts Questlove as the director says, "Watching you watch this is making me overwhelmed now. I thought I was the only person that. . . ." It is a beautiful and fitting moment because ending the film at the same place it began is a tacit acknowledgment that, like the footage, this story was never lost.

So, how could Jackson possibly come to think his memories of the Harlem Cultural Festival were figments of his imagination? How could the filmmaker, who first learned of the festival after seeing a clip of Tulchin's footage playing on a television in a restaurant in Japan, feel like the "only person" who had encountered this story?⁵ The convergence of their two different memories, coming together in shared wonder, does not confirm or deny that "Black Woodstock" took place in 1969 but rather opens onto revelations that are fundamentally intimate and affective. Stylized as a look 'behind-the-camera,'

Figure 2.1 Musa Jackson watches Hal Tulchin's footage of the Harlem Cultural Festival on an off-screen monitor during the documentary's opening sequence.

Summer of Soul mediates the shifting personal and aesthetic relations that are formed in the shared processing of history. The film records interviewees, including the percussionist Sheila E. and singers Billy Davis Jr. and Marilyn McCoo from the group The 5th Dimension as they watch the 50-year-old festival footage. Like Jackson, their reactions reflect their relationships to recorded memory. For instance, leaning forward, occasionally pointing, but never looking away from the off-screen monitor, Sheila E. intently watches and analyzes performances by Mongo Santamaria and Ray Barretto. Sheila E.'s excitement, highlighted by the color of Santamaria's set glowing in the drummer's eyeglasses, is notably a reaction to the performances and the memory of closely studying their artistry. Sheila E. explains, "I learned a lot by watching him. Ray's playing, it's all in the wrist, and that's what I learned. That's how I play." The film dramatizes the "archival reveal": set in a nondescript room (as if this is the only way to access the now-obsolete equipment needed to screen Tulchin's footage), Sheila E. re-enacts watching Barretto, and, here, she retrieves the feeling of committing a moment to memory. These scenes expose archival work – asking what we will hold on to, what we will discard, and what holds us – as primarily affective work.[6] From this perspective, a more idiosyncratic account of the festival is no less accurate or complete; in fact, it seems to confirm that there is still more historical content to be discovered, even in the case of a public memory that already exists.

Summer of Soul expresses a complex ambivalence to recording Black cultural histories that I refer to as "the Black archival impulse." In "An Archival Impulse," theorist Hal Foster identifies a tendency in contemporary art toward archival work: the gathering of extant images, objects, and texts and the presentation of these materials according to a particular system of knowledge. As a critical creative endeavor, archival art unsettles historiographic practices that have the power to both create and confirm themselves. Its aim is not to dispense with historical record keeping but rather to acknowledge the incompleteness and contingency of the archive and fill these gaps with a public culture of active participants in the technological, spatial, and aesthetic work of making memory.[7] Similarly constituted by exchanges between scholars, artists, and activists, the Black archival impulse also displays an interest in gathering around and reconsidering the readymade. However, in the specific context of blackness, these practices navigate the archive as the site of an uncomfortable proximity between *collection* – the tools and techniques that reduce Black people to objects of accumulation – and *collectivity* – the irreducibility of Black sociality. Indeed, before considering and challenging the ways an archive might articulate blackness, the Black archival impulse approaches the archive's temporalities, materialities, and modes of capture as already belonging to the epistemologies of racial difference. For instance, if an archival impulse is, as Foster suggests, "a call out to human interpretation," the Black archival impulse also calls for a reinterpretation of the discursive category of the "human" as subject to the proprietary logics of antiblackness.[8] For that reason, extending Foster's observations to Black art helps illuminate a shared feeling – specifically, an ambivalence to the archive's protections that, on one hand, offer to safeguard Black stories and, on the other, are a tool for consolidating historic and cultural value. Naming this tension, Soyica Diggs Colbert, Douglas A. Jones Jr., and Shane Vogel make the distinction between *usable* and *useful* pasts, the former describing the instrumentalization of memories as a means to an end and the latter a recognition of memories' value outside of a system of exchange.[9] As Questlove's film sets out to find a record that was never lost, it processes Tulchin's footage as a useful archive. Thus, the challenge a film like *Summer of Soul* poses to historicity is not simply a stand against its exclusions but also a call for a fundamental shift in priority. The Black archival impulse is a change in emphasis from the gathering of archival materials to the gatherings of people that coalesce around these materials.[10]

As Jackson's story implies, the Black archival impulse to explore history making as a social process designates the archive as a site for both getting together and letting go. If the Black archival impulse is to disentangle collection and collectivity, it is a sensibility that demands a reassessment of archival attachments, including fixations on completeness and objectivity, in order to clear space for experience and relation. For example, I find the end of *Summer of Soul* useful because it helps me understand my relationship to a misty memory of attending an entirely different event: the Million Man March. Like Jackson, I recall certain details that would be impossible to confirm, like the patch of grass where my family and I watched the crowd or the feel of the sunshine on my face. There are others that I could easily verify: for instance, the powerful way one speaker described the size of the crowd. And yet, I've resisted the urge to do so for almost 30 years. There is no question that for me, and possibly Jackson, putting these memories away is a gesture of self-care, a learned response to a traumatic awareness that, whether in jubilant celebration outside, quiet congregation inside, or offered as a gift to the larger community, the threat of loss looms over gatherings of Black people and Black histories.[11] Said differently, because collectivity is vulnerable to the consumptive force of collection, the Black archival impulse is to keep elusive memories, to keep memories elusive, and to find ways to gather around these unsettled pasts.[12] Denise Oliver-Velez makes this point most eloquently in *Summer of Soul* explaining, "we hold these truths to be self-evident, that Black history is gonna be erased." It is a devastating declaration, but the truth of erasure is still *ours*. In other words, together, Jackson and I know the existing archive may not be capable of verifying Black pasts, and, possibly worse, seeking verification could destroy memories that feel precious because they lack certainty. Thus, where *Summer of Soul*, Jackson, and I forgo some historical precision, we gain access to an archive of shared experience, expectation, and practices of self-preservation.

Yet, the impulse to "put memories away" seems at odds with the mediation of memory, which is the issue acknowledged in this film's subtitle, *(. . . Or, When the Revolution Could Not Be Televised)*. The subtitle is a reference to multidisciplinary artist Gil Scott-Heron's famous 1970 poem and song, "The Revolution Will Not Be Televised."[13] One of Heron's most famous works, the piece is a critique of the entwined logics of capital and visibility that denude revolutionary action when its objects and goals are limited to representation. The poem insists the fight for liberation must elude capture or, in televisual terms, be "live." It would seem *Summer of Soul*, which can be watched and rewatched on virtually any kind of screen, would contradict the point, undoing the significance Heron ascribes to events that *will not* and, in Tulchin's experience, *could not* be televised. Except, the act of recording the Harlem Cultural Festival did not guarantee the performances would be widely seen or that the festival would have a prominent place in public memory. Instead, each time the interviewees and the film appear to in some way forget what media technologies presume to remember for them, the documentary demonstrates a tension between black livingness and a static historical record. Despite the persistent claim that "liveness" in media is an "ontological condition" primarily defined by the notion of ephemerality, Philip Auslander argues liveness is "contingent, situated, and historically ductile."[14] So, in the sense that the event and footage were subject to disappearance, as a result of Black history's precarity not a lack of recording, they are still "live." By assembling experiences of forgetting and other practices of avoiding capture, the film produces a history that becomes more elusive through mediation. As a result, *Summer of Soul* does not function as a usable archive of Black history; it is, however, useful archival art about making and caring for Black histories.

"... Brothers on the Instant Replay" – Mediating the Black Archival Impulse

Between the story of the Harlem Cultural Festival and the story of its own production, *Summer of Soul* is a documentary about film making history and history making film, a slippage that acknowledges the mutuality that exists between film and history that becomes more complex under scrutiny. For instance, it is relatively easy to see the role that images, like those recorded by Tulchin and Questlove, play in producing collective memories of the past. It is also clear that these accounts both shape and are shaped by the material and cultural conditions in which these works were created, stored, and shared. For instance, *Summer of Soul* makes cinematic history amid an instant and seemingly endless stream of digital technologies that promise to remember (perhaps more accurately, collect) everything.[15] While this moment in media production is distinct, James Tobias argues every "displaced memory or desire may be *re*capitalized and streamed in dominant culture as a digital commodity, digital self, digitized experience" because these processes are *already* a part of Afro-diasporic becoming and "racialization."[16] In other words, if a complete account of a forgotten festival should in some way recall its own incompleteness, that self-awareness is a function of the expanding reach of media memory. Indeed, turning "belatedness into becomingness" is not just an impulse of contemporary Black filmmaking practices; it is an impulse of black livingness.[17] Therefore, the blurry entanglement of film making history and history making film in the documentary, similar to Jackson and me keeping our memories and the memory of their fragmentation, is not cynicism directed toward the archive or the forms of media that documents the present. Rather, it is how contemporary Black archival art "holds loss as loss."[18]

As *Summer of Soul* amasses archival alternatives that prioritize black people, it is the image of the crowd that comes to express the Black archival impulse's focus on collectivity, process its relationship to image-making, and express anticipation as a way of feeling for useful futures in the archive. In *Summer of Soul*, Jackson recalls:

> As far as I could see, it was just Black people. This is the first time I'd ever seen so many of us. It was incredible. Families, fathers, mothers, kids running around. . . . It was the ultimate Black barbeque. And then you start to hear music, and someone speaking, and you knew, it was something bigger.

Jackson describes the beauty of this "sea of Black people," and, despite its utter unfamiliarity, he already recognized the crowd image as the festival's most audacious performance. In Elias Canetti's canonical writing on the

The Black Archival Impulse 27

topic, the author argues a crowd desires constant growth that starts with discharge – members of the crowd abandoning individuality and distance – and ends with disintegration – the inevitable eruption of constant expansion.[19] Thus, somewhere between appearance and disappearance, the transitory movement that defines the festival crowd is as distinct and singular as the performances on stage. As much as "movies are crowd machines," capable

Figure 2.2 and *Figure 2.3* Close up and long shot of Harlem Cultural Festival attendees during the documentary's opening sequence.

of both imaging crowds and coalescing their own, these images maintain an elusive quality.[20] As Andrew V. Uroskie explains:

> The collective subject tends to emerge as a site of representational breakdown; it is that which cannot be representationally secured. This is why, within the tradition of artistic modernism, the crowd tends to be figured either through a kind of essential ambivalence, or else a particularly liminal kind of object – fleeting, insubstantial, transitory. And precisely because it seems to defy representation, the figure of the crowd often comes to stand in for the perceived limitations of both the practice, and the epistemology, of the particular modality or representation.[21]

These images are an archive of the kinds of loss debated in theories of the crowd – the loss of order, previous group affiliations, private property, and so on – and an already lost visual record.[22] Crowd images are essential to the storied afterlives of events like the Harlem Cultural Festival and the Million Man March. Subsequently, *Summer of Soul* uses the crowd to render the other contingencies that shape this history. For example, the intertitles that open the film appear in between images of festival attendees that alternate between long shots and close ups that occasionally catch one or two people staring directly into the camera. These chance encounters with unknown individuals and an undifferentiated crowd put the intertitles into sharper relief. They've waited patiently for a returned look. Maybe we can find them. But we also came so close to missing them. Perhaps we did. In a sense, the crowd teaches the screen image how to, using Heron's terms, "be live."

The Black archival image anticipates *more* – that more people will join, more footage will be found, and even that more footage will be lost – for that reason, it is a useful gathering point for a crowd that "exists as long as it has an unattained goal."[23] Some archival drama is, thus, a way to keep the crowd together. For instance, between festival and interview footage, *Summer of Soul* includes archival photographs and documents to which it adds the animated effect of a grease pencil circling details on a contact sheet. Like the interview with Jackson, the animated annotations emphasize the occasions in which, upon closer examination, the historical record was already there, and, thus, we can virtually guarantee that there is still more. Literally drawing attention to these moments, the documentary is not constructing or discovering an entirely different account of the event, rather it emphasizes that each record of past events is also a record of past erasure, and black cultural history is made in the process of marking both. Of course, each additional layer of mediation reproduces the quantity of archival material that, once again, is not simply the documentation but rather the enactment of the relationships to memory-making that are part of Black livingness. Accordingly, we might consider the various anachronisms in Questlove's film as instances in which

Figure 2.4 Using an animated effect that resembles a grease pencil used to edit or annotate a contact sheet, *Summer of Soul* performs the repeated gestures of archival work, marking the film's reaction to archival material.

the Black archival impulse is to gather and await the past's re-emergence in a still unknown and unfinalized future.

In *Summer of Soul*, the late cultural critic Greg Tate explains that for those who, threatened by violent erasure, are estranged from their histories and futures, Black music provides a model for this kind of transhistoric Black collectivity. Accompanying ecstatic shots of artists and audiences singing and dancing, Tate's voice-over explains:

> There's something very specific about what happened in Black America where I think the only place we could be fully expressive was in music, was in these church rituals. Gospel was channeling the emotional core of Black people. . . . There's this notion of spirit possession that comes from Africa. It's part of seeking a certain kind of release and catharsis. This is an eruption of spirit to arrive at an inner peace through being completely, expressively open.

Tending to the legacy of Black music unmooring affective histories and making them useful for future generations, *Summer of Soul* approaches the musical performances with notable restraint, avoiding heavy-handed cross-cutting and didactic voice-overs in favor of extended and largely unedited sequences. Still, *Summer of Soul*, a film directed by a famous musician, creates its own arrangements, orchestrated around the performances' various emotional charges: the wonder captured in the precision of R&B acts like Gladys Knight & the Pips and David Ruffin; the sense of gratitude and deep connection in the section that features Afro-diasporic relation in the performances of Mongo Santamaria and Ray Barretto; and the unabashed rage in the sequence that begins with Kimati Dinizulu's manic percussion section and transitions into performances by Max Roach, Abbey Lincoln, Hugh Masekela, and Nina Simone. Making moving images of moving images of moving musical performances, *Summer of Soul* treats these sounds as rhythmic refrains that, as Derek P. McCormack describes, "hold together affective, conceptual, and textual milieus as a kind of signature, or style, drawn out as a series of lines of creative variation."[24] So, at the same time each artist's performance and interviewee's story is distinct and deeply personal, *Summer of Soul* arranges cinematic forms, like its narrative frame, interview *mise-en-scène*, and animated effects, as Black archival art's affective refrains. The film joins the crowd in the assumption that these feelings will return.

The clearest example of the conjuring Tate described in the documentary occurs during the gospel sequence when Rev. Jesse Jackson leads the crowd in a prayer and, with Ben Branch and the Operation Breadbasket Orchestra and Choir, Mahalia Jackson and Mavis Staples, sings "Precious Lord, Take My Hand," Dr. Martin Luther King Jr.'s favorite song. In the film, the entire virtuosic musical performance is an incredible intergenerational exchange between the musicians; Rev. Jackson, who stands onstage with the musicians and recalls the 1968 assassination of MLK in agonizing detail; and, intercutting that archival footage, Rev. Jackson yet again, this time appearing in an interview from the present day. Together, 'they' tell the story of the day in Memphis, talking to each other as if the specific recollection – Rev. Jackson's final conversation with King – is not yet complete. Then, in the contemporary interview, Rev. Jackson yells "POW!", and at that moment the screen cuts to black and Branch's orchestra strikes a loud chord. The next shot is Joseph Louw's now-famous photograph of King lying on the balcony of the Lorraine Motel. When the image returns to the festival footage, the audience's head is bowed in prayer and the performance continues. In the past and present, Rev. Jackson is willing to give, and give again, a personal account of a profoundly traumatic event. Accordingly, the film seems to acknowledge how hard it is to hold this kind of loss. Cutting between obscure archival festival footage, the famous archival photograph, and the contemporary interview, the memory becomes a refrain. Tragically, recovery is not possible, but it is also not the only aim of archival art. Instead, in this instance, the Black archival impulse is to follow the music's "soul logic" that Emily J. Lordi describes as "a diverse and experimental set of aesthetics, which themselves express a range of ways of being black together in a perilous age."[25]

"The Revolution Will Not Be Televised": A Pre- and Post-Pandemic Media Theory

Questlove's documentary about capturing the kinetic energy of crowds and live performance premiered during a high point in a global pandemic, a particularly difficult time to, as Heron advised, "be in the street."[26] Fortunately, because of its acute awareness of media's seemingly infinite reach, the black archival impulse to assemble is not limited to certain locations or forms of collectivity. Rather, it is a commitment to making connections where they seem unfounded or otherwise ill-advised, like my own tenuous link between the Harlem Cultural Festival and the Million Man March. Still, in these movements for change, it is evident that making history and history making both take time, and that is what these crowds want. Thus, while their contexts are markedly different, whatever remains as film or video is a demand for the return of the "deleted, wounded, othered, or dead modes of historical memory" that are not just represented by these images but accrued in the apparatus.[27] Contemporary works like *Summer of Soul* invite archival tools to preserve the possibility of their own disappearance and, thus, to do crowd work. From this perspective, the revolution might not be televised, but as it uses media objects as a formal articulation of collective loss, it is televisual. Heron's song, first recorded in 1970 and again in 1971, re-emerges in Questlove's film as an enduring media theory that arrives just in time for a crisis that demands we re-evaluate our relationships to each other.

With an uncanny prescience, Heron's media theory anticipated the need to revisit archival strategies, and, in the wake of a global pandemic, we do need an archive to hold loss. Of course, it would not be the aim of this historic record to sustain suffering. The Black archival impulse is an orientation toward archival materials only as much as it is an orientation toward people. As such, the remit of an archive of archival erasure, like any other, would be uncovering the linkages between the objects, both found and lost. Similarly, when Heron claims the revolution will be live, it seems the song is describing a kind of media relation that is less about avoiding commercials and re-runs and more, given the proximity of collection and collectivity or usability and usefulness, about discovering new ways to connect people to unsettled histories. Foster similarly observes the archival impulse as desire for relation, "might archival art emerge out of a similar sense of a failure in cultural memory, of a default in productive traditions? For why else connect so feverishly if things did not appear so frightfully disconnected in the first place?"[28] Frankly, it is possible that we will forget again – about the Harlem Cultural Festival, Tulchin's footage, and Questlove's documentary. Awaiting that moment, those gathered in and around *Summer of Soul* use the imperfect historiographic tools that are always at our disposal to make audacious connections that *feel* right. We'll need them next time.

Notes

1. Later we learn this is the voice of Cyril 'Bullwhip' Innis Jr., a Black Panther party member who attended the festival.

2. "Hulu, Onyx Collective and Searchlight Pictures Present a Questlove Jawn *Summer of Soul (. . . Or, When the Revolution Could Not Be Televised)*," Pressroom, Searchlight Pictures, last modified December 14, 2022, https://press.searchlightpictures.com/summer-of-soul/.
3. Stephen Battaglio, "Meet the Archivist Who Saved the Historic Footage That Became *Summer of Soul*," *Los Angeles Times*, August 19, 2021, www.latimes.com/entertainment-arts/business/story/2021-08-19/meet-the-archivist-who-rescued-the-concert-footage-that-became-the-summer-of-soul.
4. Anthony Vidler, *The Architectural Uncanny: Essays in the Modern Unhomely* (Cambridge: MIT Press, 1992), 224.
5. Pat Ralph, "Questlove Shares How He First Saw 'Summer of Soul' Footage – But He Had No Idea What He Was Watching," *Philly Voice*, July 15, 2021, www.phillyvoice.com/questlove-summer-of-soul-film-hulu-seth-meyers-harlem-cultural-festival/.
6. This description of holding and my phrasing are inspired by Okwui Okpokwasili's 2020 performance *Sitting on a Man's Head* at Danspace Project in New York City in which "activators" participating in the performance piece were invited to answer the question, "What do you carry that also carries you?" For a brilliant discussion of Okpokwasili's artistic practice, the artist's reflections on post-COVID collaboration, and a reconceptualization of the archive that poses the question, "How do we make sure our relationship with the archive stays a dynamic one, and one where we respect that whatever we're looking at was tremulous?" see Kristin Juarez, "Within the Whirlwind of the Encounter: An Interview with Okwui Okpokwasili," *liquid blackness: journal of aesthetics and black studies* 5, no. 2 (October 2021).
7. Hal Foster, "An Archival Impulse," *October* 110 (Autumn 2004): 5.
8. Ibid.
9. Soyica Diggs Colbert, Douglas A. Jones Jr., and Shane Vogel, "Introduction: Tidying Up After Repetition," in *Race and Performance after Repetition Performance*, eds. Soyica Diggs Colbert, Douglas A. Jones Jr., and Shane Vogel (Durham, NC: Duke University Press, 2020), 22.
10. These gatherings of people should be understood broadly. For instance, viewing *Summer of Soul*, even asynchronously, is an occasion for people to connect around a historical account of black life. Further, the significance of that sociality is not contingent upon a conventional sense of historical rigor, methodology, or even accuracy.
11. Matt Zapotosky, "Charleston Church Shooter: 'I Would Like to Make It Crystal Clear, I Do Not Regret What I Did,'" *The Washington Post*, January 4, 2017, www.washingtonpost.com/world/national-security/charleston-church-shooter-i-would-like-to-make-it-crystal-clear-i-do-not-regret-what-i-did/2017/01/04/05b0061e-d1da-11e6-a783-cd3fa950f2fd_story.html; Topher Sanders, Kate Rabinowitz, and Benjamin Conarck, "Walking While Black: Jacksonville's Enforcement of Pedestrian Violations Raises Concerns That It's Another Example of Racial Profiling," *ProPublica*, November 16, 2017, https://features.propublica.org/walking-while-black/jacksonville-pedestrian-violations-racial-profiling/; Gianluca Mezzofiore, "A White Woman Called Police on Black People Barbecuing. This Is How the Community Responded," *CNN.com*, May 22, 2018, www.cnn.com/2018/05/22/us/white-woman-black-people-oakland-bbq-trnd/index.html. Jeff Tischauser, "After Patriot-Linked Vandalism, A Black Artist Searches for Vindication," *Southern Poverty Law Center*, April 17, 2023, www.splcenter.org/hatewatch/2023/04/17/after-patriot-front-linked-vandalism-black-artist-searches-vindication.
12. Further unsettling the history of the Million Man March is the event's connection to Nation of Islam leader Louis Farrakhan. Although the march was attended by prominent and respected Black activists and artists, it was nevertheless organized by Farrakhan whose record of virulently antisemitic and anti-LGBTQIA statements

stand in stark contradiction to an event with the stated purpose of demonstrating the scale of Black solidarity.
13. Gil Scott-Heron, "The Revolution Will Not Be Televised," Track #1 on *Small Talk at 125th and Lenox*, Flying Dutchman/RCA, 1970.
14. Philip Auslander, *Liveness: Performance in a Mediatized Culture*, 3rd ed. (London and New York: Routledge, 2023), 7.
15. James Tobias, "The Music Film as Essay: Montage as Argument in Khalil Joseph's *Fly Paper* and *Process*," in IN FOCUS: Modes of Black Liquidity: Music Video as Black Art, eds. Alessandra Raengo and Lauren McLeod Cramer, special issue, *Journal of Cinema and Media Studies* 59, no. 2 (Winter 2020): 157–62. Tobias explores black filmmakers' recent updates to the essay film, the loosely defined category of highly reflexive non-fiction films that address the boundaries of personal and public. These films and Tobias's study are foundational to my claims about mediated memory.
16. Tobias, "Music Film as Essay," 159.
17. Foster, "An Archival Impulse," 22.
18. Tobias, "Music Film as Essay," 160. In Tobias's essay this claim is made in conversation with Alessandra Raengo's close reading of Kahlil Joseph's *Fly Paper* (2018). See Alessandra Raengo, "Sounding Out a Stumble: Melancholic Loops in Kahlil Joseph's *Fly Paper*," in "LB Art Reviews," *liquidblackness.com*, https://liquidblackness.com/curating-for-blackness/arflypaper.
19. Elias Canetti, *Crowds and Power*, trans. Carol Stewart (New York: The Viking Press, 1962), 16–19.
20. Lesley Brill, *Crowds, Power, and Transformation in Cinema* (Detroit, MI: Wayne State University Press, 2006), 1.
21. Andrew V. Uroskie, "Far Above the Madding Crowd: The Spatial Rhetoric of Mass Representation," in *Crowds*, eds. Jeffrey T. Schnapp and Matthew Tiews (Stanford, CA: Stanford University Press, 2006), 317.
22. The evolution of crowd semantics as they appear across the discourse of film censorship and film theory ranges from pathological warnings that echo the contagion thesis propagated by early crowd psychologist Gustave Le Bon, to description of aesthetic forms that resemble novelist Elias Canetti's decidedly less alarmist and highly systematized theorization. See Brill, *Crowds, Power, and Transformation*; Schnapp and Tiews, eds. *Crowds*; Michael Tratner, *Crowd Scenes: Movies and Mass Politics* (New York: Fordham University Press, 2008).
23. Canetti, *Crowds and Power*, 29.
24. Derek P. McCormack, *Refrains for Moving Bodies: Experience and Experiment in Affective Spaces* (Durham, NC: Duke University Press, 2013), 67–68.
25. Emily J. Lordi, *The Meaning of Soul: Black Music and Resilience Since the 1960s* (Durham, NC: Duke University Press, 2020), 6.
26. In "The Revolution Will Not Be Televised" Heron declares, "Black people will be in the street looking for a brighter day" and *Summer of Soul* did, indeed, premiere at an in-person screening at the Sundance Film Festival in January 2021.
27. Tobias, "Music Film as Essay," 161.
28. Foster, "An Archival Impulse," 23.

3 Beyond Black Woodstock

Summer of Soul as Historical Recovery

Landon Palmer

In July 1969, while many American newspapers reported on the Apollo 11 moon landing, the African American newspaper *The Philadelphia Tribune* wrote of a different piece of history in the making. "While the eyes of the rest of the world were on the moon landing," wrote Art Peters, "more than 75,000 persons in Harlem ignored the lunar spectacle Sunday afternoon and rocked and rolled in the rain to the soulful sounds of some of Motown's biggest stars."[1] The event described here is the Harlem Cultural Festival, a showcase of Black music staged weekly throughout the late summer of 1969 that put on display a variety of genres, including Motown rhythm and blues, contemporary jazz, psychedelic funk, gospel, and blues, as well as Latin and African musics.

Ahmir "Questlove" Thompson's archival documentary *Summer of Soul (. . . Or, When the Revolution Could Not Be Televised)* (2021) chronicles the meanings and experiences of this event for its performers and attendees. One segment in particular illustrates the dichotomy observed by the *Tribune* story, that is, the distance between what the mainstream, white-dominated press considered newsworthy and the perspectives of the festival's predominately Black attendees. In a sequence that juxtaposes The Staple Singers' performance of "It's Been a Change" with broadcast news footage, the film introduces on-the-street reactions from white interviewees expressing awe over the moon landing, one of whom asserts, "I felt the world got closer today. I felt we all got to know each other that much more." *Summer of Soul* then pivots to interviews with Black attendees of the Harlem Cultural Festival who attest that the festival's gathering of stage performers is just as (if not more) important than the moon landing, and they critique the federal government's investment in space travel as urban poverty goes ignored. The gap in "knowing each other more" is laid bare by *Summer of Soul*, demonstrating that the events that have made up a certain canonized narrative of what "defined" the American 1960s are not universally meaningful and, in fact, obscure histories important to other groups of Americans.

In line with this critique, the historical and cultural significance of the 1969 Woodstock Music and Art Fair casts a notable shadow over *Summer of Soul*. The

DOI: 10.4324/9781003397601-4

opening title cards introduce the Harlem Cultural Festival as having occurred "during the same summer as Woodstock," which took place "100 miles" from Harlem. During *Summer of Soul*'s development and promotion, the documentary was described by media outlets as the "Black Woodstock" project, a moniker inherited from decades-long efforts by filmmakers to preserve the history of this festival in a feature film.[2] *Summer of Soul*'s framing of the Harlem Cultural Festival as a counternarrative to Woodstock – a more canonized event due to the dominance of white perspectives in chronicling the cultural history of the 1960s, its status realized in part by Michael Wadleigh's hit documentary film about the festival – makes sense as part of its mission as a corrective to a cultural memory of 1969 dominated by white experience. It is also a strategy consistent with contemporary popular music documentaries that reframe established histories as a means to recover lesser-known histories.[3] Finally, the comparison demonstrates the limits of Woodstock as an encapsulation of 1960s popular music festival culture, as *Summer of Soul* foregrounds the affordances of the Harlem Cultural Festival's distinct urban setting.

This chapter explores how *Summer of Soul* renders the Harlem Cultural Festival distinctive as a late-1960s music festival through its framing alongside Woodstock. In *Summer of Soul*'s development, narrative structure, and promotion, "Woodstock" serves as a metonym for not only the dominant cultural narratives about late-1960s popular culture events but also the prevailing tendencies of concert documentaries during this period, as exemplified by *Woodstock: Three Days of Peace and Music* (Michael Wadleigh, 1970). Through this framing, Woodstock signifies the hegemonic centrality of white perspectives in previous cultural histories of late-1960s America. *Summer of Soul* invokes Woodstock as a corrective to such annals and enlists the Harlem Cultural Festival to demonstrate what stories remain obscured as a result – an affective example of the cost of the normative recycling of history. The cost of this obscuring, as depicted in *Summer of Soul*, lies in the limited circulation of the archival footage – shot and preserved by filmmaker Hal Tulchin – that the film seeks to revive. *Summer of Soul*'s act of recovering marginalized cultural history also functions as a critique of the music documentary – specifically, the white-dominant commercial terms that have shaped the production and exhibition of concert documentaries – as Tulchin's footage of the Harlem Cultural Festival did not receive the same contemporaneous feature-length treatment as Woodstock. Where *Woodstock* augmented the cultural-historical significance of Woodstock, *Summer of Soul* offers a belated compensation for the absence of an equivalent with the Harlem Cultural Festival.

In doing so, *Summer of Soul* serves as a critique of the late-1960s direct cinema concert documentary, a genre and mode of production that privileged countercultural rock events, participated in their mythmaking, and popularized a music documentary aesthetic that served as a moving image expression of the politics of rock authenticity. The late-1960s direct cinema concert documentary constituted, as I will elaborate, a moving image manifestation of "rockism" in its stylistic approach to stage performance that augmented the status of countercultural rock festivals as exceptional events that reimagined communities. In contrast, *Summer of Soul* depicts a music festival that was embedded within the everyday. Its strategies of contextualization and the complicated legacy of its archival footage present a rethinking of concert narratives and images outside of the established (read: white) paradigm of the concert documentary genre.

Woodstock and the Direct Cinema Concert Documentary

Feature documentaries that captured late-1960s concerts and music festivals gain their power not only through their status as the authoritative interpretation of the events they depict but also via the style through which these events are captured and represented. Many such films were made as part of the direct cinema documentary movement, a nonfiction film practice that employed minimal narration and interviews in favor of observational techniques facilitated by flexible moving image and sound capture technologies. As Keith Beattie argues, direct cinema "rockumentaries" prioritize "the performing body" in their modes of display, offering viewers more than a vicarious substitute for concert attendance, but an intimate perspective on performance that can exceed what the live, in-person experience allows.[4] This focus on performance made direct cinema documentaries fit comfortably within 1960s rock music's politics of authenticity. As Philip Auslander argues, authenticity in rock culture is founded on a central contradiction: that live performance constitutes the determinative site in which talent and versatility are evaluated, yet notions of value in liveness are shaped by mediated representations.[5] Where Auslander focuses on the album as the primary referent for live performance, I have argued that depictions of rock performance in concert documentaries produced standards for what live rock is "meant" to look and sound like. This effect is augmented by the fact that direct cinema techniques convey the impression of an (often misleading) absence of interference in the performance or event itself.[6] The vast recirculation of images from these films within other nonfiction media enriched their status as the authoritative audiovisual account of their profilmic events.[7]

Late-1960s rock was widely understood in contemporaneous popular culture as a "white" genre of music despite its origins in blues and other African American music traditions and the many Black rock musicians who established the genre. Rock's visual expression in the direct cinema concert documentary meant that the established visual language and genre preferences of the most successful and well-known concert documentaries opened little space for representing events that resided outside this rock-centric paradigm.[8] Direct cinema concert documentaries served as the moving image manifestation of rockism, an ideological perspective of music that values expressions of rock authenticity as white, straight, and male. I adopt rockism here from critic

Kelefa Sanneh's conceptualization of the term in 2004. While the term did not exist during the era of the late-1960s music festival, it helps to distill the combination of aesthetic preferences and political values associated with rock that cohere in such documentaries as well as the received notions of what subject matter is important that is intrinsic to such films' distribution and reception.[9]

Michael Wadleigh's documentary of Woodstock exemplifies how such films practice rockism. Wadleigh, previously a New York–based cinematographer of underground cinema, was not a direct associate of the direct cinema movement, a group of documentarians whose careers developed under the aegis of documentarian Robert Drew. However, when the Woodstock Music and Art Fair's concert organizers solicited filmmakers to record a feature for the event (a means to recoup costs of the free festival), they interviewed D.A. Pennebaker and David and Albert Maysles in addition to Wadleigh, clearly signaling a preference for observational documentary techniques popularized by Pennebaker's *Dont Look Back* (1967) and *Monterey Pop* (1968).[10] Wadleigh's approach to filming Woodstock included many techniques associated with the direct cinema movement such as employing light, portable filmmaking equipment to ensure flexible observation of performances without disruption.[11] *Woodstock*'s handheld aesthetic (multiplied by editor Thelma Schoonmaker's inventive split-screen technique in post-production) contributed to its experiential value, giving audiences an intimate, privileged perspective of stage performances via cameras often placed immediately below the stage. Hence, Woodstock's camerawork offers an idealized perspective of stage performance that allows unfettered observation of the musicians' work. The grain of the film's 16mm capture format, rendered conspicuous when the film was blown up to 70mm for exhibition, lends *Woodstock* a decisively unpolished visual style that matches the festival's earthy setting in rural New York. Its modest production values (in contrast to Hollywood's 35mm standard) further echo the festival's improvisatory creation and countercultural ideals. *Woodstock*'s countercultural populism is also expressed in its major deviation from direct cinema: its direct interviews with festival attendees. Veering closer to the participant-observation practices of cinéma vérité, these interviews offer firsthand perspectives of "hippie" youth and the meanings of the festival to its attendees.

Notably, *Woodstock* is bookended by performances by two Black guitarists, Richie Havens and Jimi Hendrix.[12] As Jack Hamilton demonstrates, popular Black rock stars like Hendrix were largely perceived as "alien" to the white-dominant world of rock music during this period, an exception proving the rule of "a racial imagination of rock music that was quickly rendering blackness invisible, so much so that at the time of [Hendrix's] death the idea of a black man playing electric lead guitar was literally remarkable."[13] Many white rock musicians and groups such as The Rolling Stones appropriated "blackness" in their performance styles and sources of musical inspiration in service of their rock authenticity. By the late 1960s, rock's blackness became simultaneously invoked and invisible. For a musician like Havens, then, the path to renown went through white popular music, as Havens first established his career by playing covers of folk and rock songs by artists like Bob Dylan and the Beatles. Hendrix's cover of "The Star-Spangled Banner," rendered largely via a lengthy observational close-up, has endured directly because of Wadleigh's documentary, which gave the performance a climactic status as a summary statement of the festival and was placed in service of cultural memory largely authored by white filmmakers, critics, and historians.[14] In short, Hendrix's exceptional position within the structure of *Woodstock* reflects his cultural position within white-dominated rock. This performance became the sonic signature of an event whose images are populated by white bodies on and off-stage, performed by an artist whose attributed exceptionality as a Black figure in the white world of rock obscures rock's Black history.[15]

Woodstock was picked up for distribution by Warner Bros., enjoyed a heavily promoted release, and became, at that time, the highest-grossing documentary ever made. By practicing an aesthetic of authenticity through its idealized observational attention to performance, and due to *Woodstock*'s major studio backing, Wadleigh's film helped augment Woodstock's place as a lodestar in the cultural history of the late 1960s, the festival that both distilled and eclipsed all others. Due to the film's success and the festival's privileged place in cultural history, *Woodstock* points to a double erasure: both of rock's African American roots and of contemporaneous festivals for which Black performers were more central. For example, Pennebaker's footage of the 1969 Toronto Rock 'n' Roll Revival, a festival that took place a month after Woodstock and featured many Black rock artists including Little Richard, Chuck Berry, and Bo Diddley, was never picked up for theatrical distribution as a complete record of the festival; instead, individual performances had delayed theatrical or home video releases. As *Summer of Soul* indicates, the same commercial inattention applied to films of festivals showcasing contemporary Black music genres.

Summer of Soul and the Exceptional Within the Everyday

Late-1960s rock festivals were not only discussed and understood by their organizers as music events but purported to practice an alternative means of communal living, an understanding put on display in concert documentaries themselves. Mick Jagger described the rock festival in *Gimme Shelter* (David Maysles, Albert Maysles, and Charlotte Zwerin, 1970) as "a sort of microcosmic society which sets an example to the rest of America as to how one can behave in large gatherings." Woodstock organizer Artie Kornfeld is depicted telling a news crew in *Woodstock* that a festival is a place to "live together and be happy." This utopian notion of the rock festival is also a decisively rural one, wherein the space of the festival is staged outside urban markers of civilization, presenting a weekend-long retreat for the rock festival's predominately white audiences to temporarily explore this idea of community.

The Harlem Cultural Festival, by contrast, directly intersected with the everyday lives of its attendees, held over six Sundays between late June and late August within a heavily populated Black neighborhood. Thus, this festival was both part of and a momentous exception to the everyday lives of many Harlem residents. *Summer of Soul* places significant emphasis on what it was like to attend the festival via the retrospective perspectives of those who were in the crowd. The film offers witness to this unique experience of the exceptional within the everyday through interviews with several festival attendees: one, Dorinda Drake, describes the freedom she felt in walking to a festival only ten blocks away from her home, while another, Musa Jackson, coins the event as "the ultimate Black barbecue" made into "something bigger" with the live performers.

Summer of Soul benefits from Questlove's prioritization of these voices over the celebrity and expert talking heads often employed in commercial documentaries about popular music history. Such talking heads are by no means absent, but they are neither given primacy nor were they foregrounded to sell the film. For example, when Lin-Manuel Miranda makes an appearance, his presence is justified by sharing the screen with his father, Luis Miranda, a political advocate who discusses connections between Latin American and African American music cultures in Harlem. Through this emphasis on local experience, music is not depicted as a disruption or escape from everyday life, or a conceptual means for community-building. Instead, music here serves as a tool for resilience and coping in the face of racial struggle in the United States as well as a means for enacting "freedom dreams," cultural tools for experiencing pleasure and community in the face of systemic subjugation.[16]

Toward this end, *Summer of Soul* is organized around archival footage of individual performances, for which commentary is provided by the performers, attendees, or others who give insight into the legacy of songs, the cultural and political histories of genres, and how certain songs reflect Black political activism of the period. Via this strategy, the film reveals the limits of strictly observational approaches popularized by direct cinema and employs form to echo the immediate social, cultural, and political significance of the music performed onstage. For example, in a section focusing on gospel, *Summer of Soul* uses several strategies to show how the festival was linked to other aspects of African American life, such as the Pentecostal Church. *Summer of Soul* juxtaposes The Edwin Hawkins Singers' performance of "Oh Happy Day" with choir member Adrienne Kryor's talking-head commentary about the social difficulties she experienced in a Pentecostal church community after having been part of a crossover hit that might encourage listeners to dance. She discusses how the group emerged from the context of the church, an exposition that is accompanied by still photographs of the group in more church-friendly environments, as the audio of the song performance continues in the background. Her detailing of the song's adoption by San Francisco deejays connects this milieu to the song and group's popularity outside of

40 *Landon Palmer*

Pentecostal churches, bringing their music to clubs and "secular artists" prior to the Harlem Cultural Festival – the influence of the choir punctuated by footage of festival attendees singing along to the song. While "the church was upset" about this development, resulting in social marginalization for these singers, Kryor attests to fulfilling her spiritual mission toward various audiences in need. This claim is echoed by an archival interview of Edwin Hawkins stating his mission to use song to take the gospel to listeners who may not attend church during a period of social tumult and change. Hence, the film balances opportunities for audiences to enjoy the music itself with substantive

Figure 3.1 and *Figure 3.2* Archival performance footage of The Edwin Hawkins Singers at the Harlem Cultural Festival is juxtaposed with other archival materials, exemplifying *Summer of Soul*'s approach to contextualization.

historical information not self-evident on the stage. While such strategies are hardly new in popular music documentaries, *Summer of Soul*'s careful pairing of performance and exposition enriches the performance onstage with the contexts from which such performances drew meaning.

Yet, *Summer of Soul* also knows when to suspend contextualization and just let the music speak. Following the moon landing segment, the film pivots to Stevie Wonder's performance of "Shoo-Be-Doo-Be-Doo-Da-Day" onstage. We hear commentary from a contemporary interview with Wonder about the festival's positioning at a transitional moment in his biography, when he moved beyond the apolitical crossover sounds of Motown and adapted to the "change" he was sensing in the culture. Then we watch Chris Rock reflect on whether Wonder would merely recycle his earlier 1960s hits like other Motown artists or move forward with the culture in 1969. Momentarily halting this commentary, the camera then sits in awe of Wonder's entrancing keyboard solo as shots of Wonder from various angles dissolve into one another before the film transitions to an archival montage of Wonder's contemporaneous political involvement. *Summer of Soul* here employs interviews in order to inform the viewer of the meaning of performances in 1969 and then makes space for audiences to immerse themselves in observing the virtuosic music onstage.

In a similar fashion, Mahalia Jackson's performance of "Precious Lord" is introduced in relation to the assassination of Martin Luther King Jr. the year before. That King drew on this song for inspiration and resilience is revealed by Reverend Jesse Jackson Jr., who appears both in talking-head interview form and as an archival subject onstage. A still image of Dr. King's corpse appears alongside the sound of a gunshot before cutting to the archival Jesse Jackson giving a speech reflecting on King's death. Separate archival interview audio with Mavis Staples is then presented to offer her perspective on Mahalia Jackson's performance before the archival video footage shows her taking the stage in advance of Jackson. The film withholds any commentary as Mahalia Jackson commands the microphone, allowing close-ups of her impassioned performance of "Precious Lord" to unfold without interruption.

This formal choice (re)opens the spiritual space for reflection, uplift, and mourning for which the original performance served. It is in these moments that *Summer of Soul* may come to resemble direct cinema techniques of idealized observation of stage performances. However, where the direct cinema concert documentary stages such performances as a means of immersing oneself in the festival's utopian space of sound and images, the performances in *Summer of Soul* are framed as an expression of historical events and political developments offstage. The talking-head interviews serve to further the work of the festival itself, to establish the festival space as one not of retreat, but as a site for relief, voice, uplift, and community for the festival's audience on the very streets in which Harlemites struggle, remember, and come together. That *Summer of Soul*'s archival footage uses fewer close-ups than *Woodstock* (several of the original production's cameras are clearly set up some distance from the stage) offers a community-focused alternative to privileged observation from the front row, reminding the film audience that there is no festival without this crowd, this neighborhood, this context. *Summer of Soul*'s inventive montages further connect onstage performances to offstage phenomena from the moon landing to the growth of Afrocentric fashion. Via such approaches, *Summer of Soul* places its audience in a layered space of reflection on both the festival and its meanings within the everyday lives of its attendees.

The Materiality of *Summer of Soul*

The material manifestation of this archival performance footage on video is intrinsic not only to the experiential immediacy of *Summer of Soul* but also to the film's claims of importance. In capturing the festival, Tulchin and his crew implemented video technologies instead of the concert documentary's 16mm standard and, as previously mentioned, often placed their cameras further from the stage than the onstage or pit-based perspective facilitated in direct cinema documentaries. The resulting (and remastered) footage is smooth and colorful, preserving the vibrancy of the Harlem Cultural Festival's stage design and its performers in full view via the vicarious positioning of the cameras. The neon green dresses donned by The Edwin Hawkins Singers, for instance, help generate a festival aesthetic that contrasts Woodstock's earthly tones. Questlove thankfully does not force the Academy ratio footage into his 16:9 frame, and the presence of soft edges on the horizontal sides of the frame gives it a raw quality, as if we are watching it through an analog editing monitor or seeing it projected onto a distant wall. This in-the-archive approach becomes part of the documentary itself, as Questlove cues up footage to trigger the memories of the attendees and performers he interviews. The light of the images reflects onto the subjects' faces, as if providing a visual illustration of their subjective travel back to this moment, a resurrection of something that existed only in memory to the status of visible evidence.

Eventually, *Summer of Soul* gives direct attention to the provenance of this footage. The film features a montage of still images displaying the aftermath of the festival, where litter occupies the grass in place of people (an echo of *Woodstock*'s ending). This is followed by images evincing untouched cartridges of videotape and reel-to-reel audiotape over archival audio of the late Tulchin discussing his failure to sell a "Black Woodstock." The Black Woodstock label "didn't help," Tulchin's voice explains, "Nobody was interested in the Black show. Nobody! Nobody cared about Harlem." Distributors, Tulchin's archival audio attests, did not see Black music as making for a marketable nonfiction motion picture commodity akin to (white) countercultural rock. Within this cultural absence lies *Summer of Soul*'s purpose to restore a history long forgotten by white capitalism, to utilize the economy of 2020s documentary production to resurrect cultural memory of an important music event lost within late-1960s documentary economics.

While this moment of the film resonates urgently regarding the common erasure and marginalization of Black cultural history, *Summer of Soul*'s claims – in both the film and its promotion – that such footage simply lay dormant for half a century have been overstated. Over decades, several filmmakers sought to make a version of this documentary and, contrary to *Summer of Soul*'s second title, (. . . *Or, When the Revolution Could Not Be Televised)*, Tulchin's footage was distributed for local television broadcasts across the country and abroad. Tulchin's original intention for his footage was to edit it into four television episodes to be broadcast across consecutive weekends in a fashion that resembles the schedule of the festival itself. According to music journalist Lily Moayeri, at least two such episodes aired in at least 15 American media markets in 1969, as television coverage in local newspapers evinces.[17] Local broadcasts of footage from the Harlem Cultural Festival could thus be experienced similarly to the festival itself: as an ephemeral series of nearby showcases that were part of audiences' everyday lives, not a singular event that constituted a decisive break from ordinary life via a journey to a rural festival or movie theater. Tulchin also licensed these episodes to ABC Worldwide Syndication, which led to their broadcast in multiple countries, including Denmark, where archivist Joe Lauro encountered a 16mm print.[18] Lauro digitally restored Tulchin's masters circa 2004 and, over the next few years, endeavored to make a never-realized feature film from this footage with Robert Gordon and Morgan Neville, buttressed by journalistic coverage of the "discovery" of such footage.[19] The impetus for *Summer of Soul*'s existence is the fact that Tulchin's footage had not yet been turned into a feature film that could serve as an authoritative record of the event and an experiential moving-image text confirming its historical value.

The problem was not – as the film claims – that Tulchin's footage was never seen but rather that it was never *remembered* according to the traditional terms of memorializing important events in 1960s American popular culture. *Summer of Soul* speaks to how deeply cultural memory of 1960s popular music festivals is bound to the form of the feature-length documentary. Despite that a series of multiple broadcasts would suggest a more fitting resemblance to the festival itself, the circulation of Tulchin's footage on television over decades is tantamount, from *Summer of Soul*'s perspective, to forgetting due to the ephemerality of broadcasting and the absence of a centralized, authoritative text in the mold of *Woodstock* – a problem that the very existence of *Summer of Soul* sets out to resolve. The significance of an authoritative, singular feature-length documentary of a music festival is a received tenet of the canonized 1960s concert documentary that *Summer of Soul* does not challenge. In film magazines of the 1970s, several direct cinema documentarians and proponents heralded direct cinema feature filmmaking as an authentically cinematic approach to documentary that draws from the medium's history and furthers its potential.[20] Such writing elided direct cinema's own roots in television, particularly via the inciting work of Robert Drew. Indeed, *Monterey Pop* began as a television project.[21] In ignoring the television history of Tulchin's footage, *Summer of Soul* misses an opportunity to explore how the relative cultural capital attributed to cinema obscures how other media can open up alternative approaches to understanding music festivals as something other than distinct, singular, autonomous events.

Conclusion

Feature-length concert documentaries have allowed certain 1960s popular music festivals to endure in cultural memory. Films like *Monterey Pop*, *Woodstock*, and *Gimme Shelter* have facilitated authoritative, canonized interpretations of the 1960s popular music festival as a distinct, sovereign event. In so doing, such films echo the contemporaneous perspective of the rural rock festival as the only space to envision an alternative model of society based in the ideals of the 1960s counterculture. They proffer the vast, empty spaces outside of major cities as proving grounds for enacting social alternatives, but only within the limits of the festival's duration.[22]

The 1969 Harlem Cultural Festival clearly did not fit within this documentary framework in its setting, temporality, approach to genre, and technological means of capture. Rather than a utopian alternative vision of society practiced in rural America on a single occasion, the Harlem Cultural Festival took place in Harlem itself over several weekends throughout the summer in which acts were organized by genre, rendering the festival a third space within the city that was integrated into urban space and offered a means for freedom-dreaming. Rather than propagating a particular genre of music or a unitary vision of counterculture, the Harlem Cultural Festival's acts were connected by a global sense of musical blackness, a diasporic understanding of Black musical traditions that fit within emerging conceptualizations of blackness in post-Civil Rights America.[23] Finally, the film rejects the intimate performer-focused perspective of the direct cinema concert documentary, preferring to place the viewer in a position that foregrounds the music's meaning from the standpoint of the Harlem community.

The framing of *Summer of Soul* around *Woodstock* makes sense as a strategy to mobilize cultural memory of a seemingly forgotten event by reference to a remembered one. The decades-long absence of a definitive feature film of the Harlem Cultural Festival comparable to *Woodstock* betrays how films such as *Woodstock* have monopolized cultural imagination of what late-1960s music festivals were, what they looked like, and who was in attendance. Rather than undermining the urgency of a film like *Summer of Soul*, the decentralized and fragmented circulation of Tulchin's footage on television and the heretofore failed attempts to transform said footage into a feature film speaks to the rockist political economy of concert documentaries and their canonization. Beyond "Black Woodstock," footage of the Harlem Cultural Festival should provoke questions of what this canonization has left out as well as other ways to imagine the meaning, significance, and form of the 1960s popular music festival through its representations. While *Summer of Soul* perpetuates the notion that television is less valuable as a platform for reclaiming cultural events, its status as a feature film offers a corrective narrative in the very same arena in which white cultural histories of the late 1960s have been elevated. Demonstrating how *Summer of Soul*'s feature film existence allowed the Harlem Cultural Festival to compete on Woodstock's terrain, both *Summer of Soul* and *Woodstock* won the Academy Award for Best Documentary Feature. Instead of challenging the medium through which musical events are conveyed in documentary form, *Summer of Soul* seeks to expand this generic canon and argues for the importance of preserving marginalized cultural histories. The film ends with a moving illustration of the personal cost of living in a culture that exhaustively returns to only a small selection of white-dominant cultural events in recounting "the Sixties." Tearing up, attendee Musa Jackson states that the footage provides "confirmation that what I knew is real," as if waking up from being gaslit by recycled images of 1969 that do not include his lived experience. This final note serves as a testament that those for whom the festival meant more than the moon landing weren't wrong – that the events which have made up African American cultural history are important, without comparison.

Notes

1. Art Peters, "75,000 Miss Moon Landing; Rock in Rain to Motown 'Soul' Music," *Philadelphia Tribune*, July 26, 1969, 22.
2. Brent Lang, "Questlove to Make Directorial Debut with 'Black Woodstock'," *Variety*, December 2, 2019, https://variety.com/2019/film/news/questlove-ahmir-thompson-black-woodstock-documentary-1203420841/; Stephen Battaglio, "Meet the Archivist Who Saved the Historic Footage That Became 'Summer of Soul'," *Los Angeles Times*, August 19, 2021, https://www.latimes.com/entertainment-arts/business/story/2021-08-19/meet-the-archivist-who-rescued-the-concert-footage-that-became-the-summer-of-soul.
3. I have written elsewhere on how contemporary music documentaries revive past historical subjects in Landon Palmer, "Strategies of the Popular Music Documentary's Recovery Mode," in *Reclaiming Popular Documentary*, eds. Christie Milliken and Steve F. Anderson (Bloomington: Indiana University Press, 2021), 259–76.
4. Keith Beattie, "It's Not Only Rock and Roll: 'Rockumentary,' Direct Cinema, and Performative Display," *Australasian Journal of American Studies* 24, no. 2 (December 2005): 21–41.
5. Philip Auslander, *Liveness: Performance in a Mediatized Culture*, 2nd ed. (New York: Routledge, 2008), 91.
6. Landon Palmer, "The Portable Recording Studio: Documentary Filmmaking and Live Album Recording, 1967–1969," *iaspm@journal* 6, no. 2 (2016): 49–69. Direct cinema documentaries were often intimately involved with the economies of certain late-1960s festivals. Organizers of festivals including Woodstock, the 1969 Rock and Roll Revival, and the Altamont Free Concert enlisted documentary productions in hopes of recouping on their investments in creating these sometimes-free events. Indeed, the selection of the Altamont Speedway for the latter festival

was decided in part due to the terms by which venues agreed to having a film crew; the infrastructure of this event (namely the inadequacies of the stage's placement) contributed to the crowd's unrest at what became an infamous concert due to a tragic murder. See Landon Palmer, *Rock Star/Movie Star: Power and Performance in Cinematic Rock Stardom* (New York: Oxford University Press, 2020), 96–134.

7. Footage from *Woodstock* is recycled in numerous feature documentaries, including *The Kids Are Alright* (Jeff Stein 1979), *Grass* (Ron Mann 1999), *My Generation* (Thomas Haneke and Barbara Kopple 2000), *Janis: Little Girl Blue* (Amy Berg 2015), and *Woodstock 99: Peace, Love, and Rage* (Garret Price, 2021), as well as many nonfiction television programs. Brian Winston writes, "The hand-held casual aesthetic of Direct Cinema meshed perfectly with the anarchic oppositional world of rock." Brian Winston, *Lies, Damn Lies and Documentaries* (London: British Film Institute, 2000), 52.
8. Jack Hamilton, *Just Around Midnight: Rock and Roll and the Racial Imagination* (Cambridge, MA: Harvard University Press, 2016), 2–8.
9. Kelefa Sanneh, "The Rap Against Rockism," *The New York Times*, October 31, 2004, www.nytimes.com/2004/10/31/arts/music/the-rap-against-rockism.html.
10. Dale Bell, *Woodstock: An Inside Look at the Movie That Shook Up the World and Defined a Generation* (Studio City, CA: Michael Wiese Productions, 1999), 44, 53; Michael Lang and Holly George-Warren, *The Road to Woodstock* (New York: HarperCollins, 2009), 147–48.
11. Bell, *Woodstock*, 13, 20.
12. Further complicating the white maleness of Woodstock's reputation as a rock event, the festival featured several performances by important women musicians of the period, including Janis Joplin, Jefferson Airplane, and Joan Baez: the former two acts were cut from the film's initial theatrical release.
13. Hamilton, *Just Around Midnight*, 2–3.
14. See Michael D. Dwyer, *Back to the Fifties: Nostalgia, Hollywood Film, and Popular Music of the Seventies and Eighties* (New York: Oxford University Press, 2015), 45–49.
15. Hamilton, *Just Around Midnight*, 2–8.
16. Robin D. G. Kelley, *Freedom Dreams: The Black Radical Imagination* (Boston, MA: Beacon Press, 2002), 11.
17. Lily Moayeri, "Actually, the Revolution WAS Televised," *Book & Film Globe*, July 29, 2021, https://bookandfilmglobe.com/film/summer-of-soul-lost-footage/.
18. Ibid.
19. Richard Morgan, "The Story Behind the Harlem Cultural Festival Featured in 'Summer of Soul'," *Smithsonian Magazine*, July 8, 2021, www.smithsonianmag.com/history/black-woodstock-summer-of-soul-146793268/.
20. Patricia Jaffe, "Editing Cinéma Verité," *Film Comment* 3, no. 3 (Summer 1965): 43; Richard Leacock, "For an Uncontrolled Cinema," *Film Culture* 22–23 (1961): 23–25.
21. Keith Beattie, *D.A. Pennebaker* (Champaign: University of Illinois Press, 2011), 41–42.
22. Stanley Booth, "*Gimme Shelter*: The True Adventures of Altamont," *Criterion*, December 1, 2009, www.criterion.com/current/posts/104-gimme-shelter-the-true-adventures-of-altamont.
23. Peniel E. Joseph, "Historians and the Black Power Movement," *OAH Magazine of History* 22, no. 3 (July 2008): 8–15.

4 A Secret History of the Secret History of the 1969 Harlem Cultural Festival

Summer of Soul, The Staple Singers, and the Rockumentary Genre

Anthony Kinik

Summer of Soul (... Or, When the Revolution Could Not Be Televised), Ahmir "Questlove" Thompson's remarkable, Academy Award–winning documentary, is first and foremost a secret history of the 1969 Harlem Cultural Festival and its contexts – that's the way it was marketed, and that's the way it announces itself in its opening minutes. It encompasses everything from the assassination of Martin Luther King Jr. on April 4, 1968, and the riots and turmoil that ensued; the Apollo 11 mission and the moon landing on July 20, 1969; and the Woodstock Music and Art Fair that took place on August 15–18, 1969, but somehow managed to overshadow its cousin to the south. But, most importantly, it's a film that clearly positions the festival as one of the premier events of the Black liberation movement that swept the United States and beyond in the 1960s and 1970s, and that incorporated interventions and actions that were political, economic, and cultural – often simultaneously. Though, like Woodstock, it featured many of the greatest musical acts of the day and attracted hundreds of thousands of spectators, the event remained little more than a rumor until *Summer of Soul* was released in 2021. "Nobody ever heard of the Harlem Cultural Festival," a disembodied voice states in the opening minutes of the film, as the audience is presented with outtakes of the scene in Harlem's Mount Morris Park for the first time in crisp, highly saturated video images. "Nobody would believe it happened."[1] The festival was witnessed by thousands of people, it was extensively videotaped for posterity, and yet it was still somehow erased from the record.[2] Moments later, a series of titles makes clear that this is a work of cultural archaeology:

> In 1969, during the same summer as Woodstock, a different music festival took place 100 miles away./Over 300,000 people attended the summer concert series known as the Harlem Cultural Festival. It was free to

DOI: 10.4324/9781003397601-5

all. The festival was filmed. But after that summer, the footage sat in a basement for 50 years. It has never been seen. Until now.

The idea that this material had "never been seen" may be a bit of overstatement,[3] but what's clear is that if Questlove sets out to reach a full understanding of how this "Soul Festival" came to be, and what it meant at the time, he also wants to come to terms with how it was made to disappear.

At the same time, *Summer of Soul* is also one of the most ambitious "rockumentaries," or popular music documentaries, in the history of the genre. Critics tended to refer to the film as a "concert movie," but the film is decidedly a festival film, with all the variety and the complexity that term implies, one that stands alongside the very greatest examples of this sub-genre, films like Bert Stern and Aram Avakian's *Jazz on a Summer's Day* (1959), Murray Lerner's *Festival* (1967), D.A. Pennebaker's *Monterey Pop* (1968), and, indeed, Michael Wadleigh's *Woodstock* (1970), and one that stands apart from tour films like Pennebaker's *Dont Look Back* (1967) and concert movies like Jonathan Demme's *Stop Making Sense* (1984).[4] Whereas the term "concert movie" suggests a single act, a single stage, and a single performance, a music festival is a considerably more complex affair with many more components, and those filmmakers who have focused their energies on them have tended to produce films with a revue-like form (usually one or two songs per act), that often address the event's origins, its logistics, and its denouement or its aftermath, and that pay a considerable amount of attention to the culture of the event and especially its large, frequently diverse audience. Even relatively recent festival films, like Jonathan Caouette's anarchic, heavily crowd-sourced *All Tomorrow's Parties* (2009), adhere to these basic parameters. *Summer of Soul* is in fact so ambitious, so virtuosic, and so highly acclaimed – along with *Woodstock*, it's just one of a small number of popular music documentaries to have won the Academy Award for Best Documentary Feature Film[5] – that a multitude of perspectives could be used to study it. Indeed, the present collection is testament to the film's rich, intricate, and captivating nature.

If, as we have seen, Questlove's film insists that the Harlem Cultural Festival was eclipsed by Woodstock, it also provokes a comparison both with its bucolic sibling festival to the north and with the Oscar-winning film that was made about it, in part because one of *Summer of Soul*'s featured acts, Sly and the Family Stone, performed at both festivals and scorching versions of "I Want to Take You Higher" can be found in both films. In fact, as Hal Tulchin, the producer who originally shot the Harlem Cultural Festival on spec, explains late in *Summer of Soul*, he started calling the project the "Black Woodstock" because this was deemed the best way to try to sell the project, and when Questlove eventually became involved, he kept "Black Woodstock doc" as his working title as we see clearly marked on the slate in the film's opening shot. But, here, following Questlove's lead, I want to take a different approach, one befitting "a different music festival," and one inspired by his modus operandi. In his book *Music Is History*, released the same year as his film, Questlove explained his goal as follows: "to chart history through music and to trace music through history, all the while trying to look more closely and more critically, trying to unreel and uncover, and to encourage readers... to do the same."[6] Thus, this chapter will situate *Summer of Soul* within the history of the rockumentary, by examining in detail the momentous onstage appearance of The Staple Singers, and especially that of Mavis Staples, during the film's "meaty gospel passage" quite specifically.[7] A number of critics have noted that Mavis Staples's duet with Mahalia Jackson on "Take My Hand, Precious Lord," performed as part of an extended tribute to Martin Luther King Jr., stands as the climax of the film. Critic Wesley Morris took things even further, declaring:

> It's an extraordinary event not just of musical history. It's a mind-blowing moment of *American* history. And for five decades, the footage of it apparently just sat in a basement, waiting for someone like Thompson to give it its due [emphasis in the original].[8]

Morris is never specific about why he finds this performance so monumental, but I would like to suggest a lot of it has to do with Mavis Staples and the presence of her family. The Staple Singers appear repeatedly in *Summer of Soul*, they stand among the film's most featured artists, and Mavis Staples is also one of its most in-demand commentators, even if she's never pictured and only addresses the audience in voice-over. What has thus far gone unremarked upon is that The Staple Singers played a similarly important role in the history of the rockumentary, having appeared in five of the genre's most significant films: Murray Lerner's *Festival* (1967), Denis Sanders's *Soul to Soul* (1971), Mel Stuart's *Wattstax* (1973), Martin Scorsese's *The Last Waltz* (1978), and now *Summer of Soul*.

Questlove's film invites its audience to revisit the early history of the so-called rockumentary and to reconsider it – especially *Woodstock*, of course, but also the entire "classical" period between 1967 and 1978, when a number of seminal films that helped establish and define the genre were released. Perhaps because of the genre's nickname, early scholarship on the popular music documentary was overly rock-centric and frequently failed to acknowledge its heterogeneity. Obviously, there's no question that rock & roll was a crucial part of the cultural zeitgeist of the 1960s and 1970s, when the popular musical documentary first emerged as a genre, but so were other musical styles, and early examples of these films – like *Jazz on a Summer's Day* (1959), *T.A.M.I. Show* (1964), and *Festival* (1967), to name just a few – encompassed jazz, gospel, folk, country, bluegrass, blues, rhythm & blues, and soul, as well as rock & roll. Placing one's attention on the role played by The Staple Singers during this period highlights a number of films that showcased musical diversity. Taking things further and focusing on the films where The Staples were integral to the overall narrative, where they made more than merely a cameo appearance, bring to light three festival films that stand as popular expressions of the Black Arts Movement, its "cultural revolution in art and ideas," and its themes of Black beauty, pride, self-determination, and justice: *Soul to Soul*, which was shot primarily in Ghana in 1971; *Wattstax*, which was photographed in Los Angeles in 1972; and *Summer of Soul*, whose principal footage was shot in Harlem in 1969.[9] Firebrands like Ron Neal and LeRoi Jones/Amiri Baraka who spearheaded the Black Arts Movement tended to "dismiss popular music . . . as trivial or corrupted," but, as Amy Abugo Ongiri has pointed out, one of the movement's articles of faith "was the belief that African American music was the preeminent example of Black aesthetic production," and the commodification of Black Power in the realm of popular culture facilitated the work of the Black Panthers and other radicals "against the state but also its absorption by it."[10] In any case, two of these films document festivals that were conceived as "Black Woodstocks," two of them document festivals that were nicknamed the "Black Woodstock," all three document festivals that have never gotten the attention they deserve – none more shamefully than the Harlem Cultural Festival – and, because of this, they've never been discussed together, in spite of the powerful connections between them.[11]

One question we might ask is what is it about The Staple Singers during this period that made them so central to this group of films? Though the group was generally characterized as a gospel act, their sound was always unique, always hard to place, somehow out of time, distinct from the mainstream of gospel music at the time. Formed in Chicago in the late 1940s, and led by Roebuck "Pops" Staples, a Mississippi native who moved north as part of the Great Migration in the 1930s, The Staple Singers were a family group known for their often sparse and haunting sound, their legendary harmonizing, and the prodigious talents of Mavis Staples, the youngest member of the group, but the one whose husky contralto was often the group's featured element. The Staple Singers went through a couple of arrangements – Pops, his son Pervis, and his daughters Cleotha and Mavis throughout most of the group's early history, Pops and his daughters Cleotha, Yvonne, and Mavis from 1969 until they disbanded in the 1990s – but they were also constantly reinventing themselves, constantly forming new alliances: with the Civil Rights Movement, the folk community, the soul scene, the Black Power contingent, and later even with disco and new wave. There's a reason The Staple Singers showed up in so many early rockumentaries – "listen to our music," Pops told Mavis. "You will hear every kind of music in our songs."[12] But there's also a reason their role in this early history has so frequently been overlooked – for decades scholars had a tendency to focus on white acts like Bob Dylan, The Beatles, The Rolling Stones, and The Band.[13] Here, too, *Summer of Soul* helps to set the record straight. In what follows, I explore The Staple Singers' appearances in *Soul to Soul*, *Wattstax*, and *Summer of Soul*, all three of which capture The Staple Singers during their Stax-era phase, when they were at the height of their popularity and influence. What we find is a musical act that embodies so many of the currents that were coursing through the Black Arts Movement at the time: the Civil Rights Movement and its radicalization; Afro-centrism; pan-Africanism; Black Power; and, tying it all together, gospel music as a cultural form that had been a central and defining part of the African American experience since the days of slavery, and one that continued to connect with the very soul of the Black community. In all three films, it is this nexus which the filmmakers mobilize, and it is how The Staple Singers are positioned and framed that holds the key to the powerful impact of these performances.

Soul to Soul (1971)

Less than two years after their appearance at the 1969 Harlem Cultural Festival, The Staple Singers were involved in another momentous and star-studded festival. The Soul to Soul Festival took place in one marathon event on March 6, 1971, in Accra, Ghana, timed to commemorate the 14th anniversary of Ghana's independence, and the star-studded line-up included Wilson Pickett, Santana, Ike & Tina Turner, Les McCann, and Roberta Flack.[14] Under the leadership of Kwame Nkrumah, the people of Ghana had discarded the colonial name the Gold Coast and become the first sub-Saharan African country to declare their independence from a colonial power – in this case, the British Empire.[15] The Gold Coast had been systematically exploited by a succession of European colonizers since the late 15th century, but, crucially, it was one of the most important centers of the transatlantic slave trade.[16] That a group of American musicians, most of whom were the descendants of slaves, were visiting one of the principal embarkation sites for the middle passage made the event highly uncanny. There they "discovered the sources of the music, rhythms, and dances" that had somehow survived through hundreds of years of separation.[17] Meanwhile, their Ghanaian hosts and fellow musicians discovered to what extent their culture had undergone transformation in the New World, having been "amalgamated with white and Latin idioms."[18] This was the full significance of the festival's and the film's name: Soul to Soul, one form of soul coming into contact with another, or, rather, two forms of soul being re-united in the motherland.

The Staple Singers' portion of *Soul to Soul* begins with the musicians Les McCann and Roberta Flack being shaken by a visit to a slave castle on the coast of Ghana. As they tour the castle's haunted spaces, McCann talks about experiencing "flashbacks," while Flack comments on the site's oppressiveness. Flack begins singing the protest spiritual "Oh, Freedom," with its haunting refrain "And before I'll be a slave/I'll be buried in my grave," and its message of deliverance through death and rebirth.[19] In this moment, a slave song that had become a crucial part of the freedom songs repertoire of the Civil Rights Movement in the 1950s and 1960s is brought back to one of the slave trade's points of origin, this coincidence of sound and space recorded on the spur of the moment on a portable tape recorder.[20] The scene ends with shots of fishermen fighting waves in a large canoe, and it is here that we begin to hear the distinctive sound of Pops Staples's tremolo-heavy guitar.

The film cuts to the festival stage, and we find The Staple Singers performing "When Will We Get Paid." The band had first appeared on film in *Festival*, where they played to a largely preppy audience at the Newport Folk Festival in 1964 wearing the suits and choir gowns that were their signature style at the time. Since then, they had signed to Memphis-based Stax Records in 1968, and with the guidance of Al Bell, the label's co-owner, The Staple Singers had reinvented themselves as a "conscious" gospel-soul act with an ear for the modern sound.[21] Bell's feel for the group's sound and their convictions, and his insistence that they record with him in Muscle Shoals, Alabama led to The Staple Singers' biggest successes: songs like "Heavy Makes You Happy (Sha-Na-Boom-Boom)," "Respect Yourself," and, especially, "I'll Take You There," their first *Billboard* Hot 100 #1 hit.[22] These sessions, which began in 1970, were "nothing short of ecstatic," and for the first time in their 20-year career, The Staple Singers were hip – funky even – and they were reaching a whole new audience. In *Soul to Soul*, Pops Staples looks relaxed in his beige vest and brown shirt, and, with Pervis no longer a part of the group, his three daughters – Cleotha, Yvonne, and Mavis – show off their "natural" hairdos, their African tie-dyed dresses, and their choreographed moves.

What's important, however, is the choice of song. "When Will We Get Paid" was one of the group's most powerful "message" songs, one which starts off by proudly boasting of the immense contributions made by African Americans to the building of the nation, but does not shy away from addressing the horrors of slavery, and ends with a forceful demand for reparations. Here, in Black Star Square in Accra, the song took on even greater meaning, reaching a climax when they hit the third and final verse and Mavis sings about the blood, sweat, and tears shed over the course of "300 years" of servitude, as well as the pain of cultural genocide. And as the song reaches its conclusion, Mavis turns her attention back to contemporary America and, with a considerable amount of disgust, questions whether African Americans will ever be accepted and will ever truly feel proud "of 'My Country, 'Tis of Thee'." It's a shattering performance, one that surely set off reverberations among those who had the opportunity to see *Soul to Soul* at the time of its release, and one that continues to resonate to this day.

Wattstax (1973)

In 1973, The Staple Singers appeared in *Wattstax*, a documentary about the elaborate concert that was put on to cap the 1972 Watts Summer Festival and commemorate the seventh anniversary of the Watts Riots. Self-consciously designed to be a Black Woodstock – a festival that would be a cultural phenomenon of the magnitude as Woodstock but would be explicitly more political than its precursor, promoting a Black nationalist agenda – the entire Wattstax project was an enormous, carefully organized undertaking, one that was staged in the Los Angeles Coliseum in front of an audience of some 100,000 spectators.[23] It united an impressive array of musicians – Eddie Floyd, Albert King, The Bar-Kays, Carla and Rufus Thomas, Isaac Hayes, and others – with numerous other Black celebrities from the realms of culture and politics: the actor Richard Roundtree, the director Melvin Van Peebles, the bandleader Billy Eckstine, and the Reverend Jesse Jackson, among them.[24] As the event's name suggests, the Wattstax concert was largely the brainchild of Al Bell. In addition to continuing to forward the Black agenda through music, capitalizing on the phenomenal success of Isaac Hayes and *Shaft*, and promoting the rest of the Stax roster, Bell wanted to get involved in film and television and so decided to set up a spectacular show in Los Angeles to make his intentions known while simultaneously generating the material for a documentary film and some record releases.[25] David Wolper, the seasoned Hollywood veteran, was hired to produce the film, and he, in turn, hired his longtime associate Mel Stuart to direct.[26] Stuart's biggest claim to fame at the time was *Willy Wonka & the Chocolate Factory* (1971), but previous to that he was primarily known as a documentarian specializing in historical and political topics. Despite this lack of Black representation at the very top of the film's production team, it was important to Bell and others at Stax that this film be used as an opportunity to hire and train local Black workers to help build a Black film and media community, so they scoured the community to create several predominantly Black crews who were sent out into the streets of Watts to capture its street life, its murals, and its architecture.[27] Meanwhile, Bell hired Wally Heider, who'd been the sound man for the Monterey Pop Festival in 1967 and the Soul to Soul Festival in 1971, to be in charge of sound at Wattstax.[28] Heider's recordings using a state-of-the-art sound system resulted in two double albums and a series of singles for Stax.[29]

The Staple Singers only perform one song onstage in *Wattstax* – their biggest release from 1971, "Respect Yourself."[30] Their performance comes about a third of the way into the film, the final act in a long opening passage that includes a half-hearted version of "The Star-Spangled Banner" (followed by a discussion of how Watts's residents feel alienated from their own country); Jesse Jackson delivering a blessing and a fiery rendition of the National Black Litany ("I Am Somebody!"), before introducing the former Motown star Kim Weston and her stirring version of the Black National Anthem (James Weldon Johnson's "Lift Every Voice and Sing"); followed by a gospel showcase that includes performances by Jimmy Jones and The Rance Allen Group, as well as a tour of the Black churches of Watts, their significance to the culture, and the passionate musical performances that can be found within. Of these, "Lift Every Voice and Sing" is particularly notable for the way it begins with Jackson and Weston leading the audience at the Coliseum in song but soon

Figure 4.1 The Staple Singers perform "Respect Yourself" in *Wattstax*.

transitions to a provocative montage sequence that includes images of slavery and Jim Crow oppression, of Black leaders and heroes (Marcus Garvey, Muhammad Ali, Frederick Douglass, Louis Armstrong, Malcolm X, Angela Davis, and so on), of protest and conflict and police brutality, before ending with shots of dignitaries gathered at the funeral of Martin Luther King Jr. and a clip of King delivering his "I've Been to the Mountaintop" speech in Memphis on April 3, 1968, the day before he was assassinated.

Within this super-charged context, Melvin Van Peebles steps onstage, reminds the audience, "[we're] here to commemorate a revolution that started the Movement and was one of the milestones in Black pride," and introduces "one of the most popular groups in the nation, The Staple Singers!" Pops, sporting an all-white, wide-lapelled leisure suit, and his daughters, now wearing chic brown sleeveless dresses with plenty of gold jewelry, launch into the song. Aside from the absence of Yvonne, who was ill and unable to perform, this rendition of "Respect Yourself" is classic Stax-era Staple Singers, with a talented and funky band backing them up, and Mavis delivering her trademark growl by the second verse.[31] Throughout the performance, the camerawork alternates between shots of The Staples onstage and shots of the fashion and the hairstyles found among the festival attendees in the bleachers. However, as Mavis finishes the second verse and the group moves into the chorus again, another montage sequence testifies to the strength of Black pride in Watts: Afro-centric murals, the Watts Festival parade, the Miss Watts beauty pageant, a Black Santa surrounded by local kids, Malcolm X College, the Harlem Hospital Center's Martin Luther King Jr. Pavilion, and so on. This sequence may not have the impact of the one that accompanied "Lift Every Voice and Sing," but it intensifies the politics of the song, and it underlines the relevance of its message to the realities of Watts and other inner cities in the early 1970s. Music scholar Rob Bowman refers to *Wattstax* as a film that "remains one of the finest examples of social commentary involving music on celluloid," and Stuart's treatment of "Respect Yourself" is one of the reasons why.

Summer of Soul (2021)

Though it was released nearly 50 years after *Wattstax*, the focus of *Summer of Soul* was the Harlem Cultural Festival in 1969, which preceded the events we see in *Soul to Soul* and *Wattstax*. It was the first time since they had signed to Stax records just a year earlier, that The Staple Singers appeared on camera – in this case on video, and not on film – and they were now in a new configuration, with Yvonne replacing Pervis for the first time.[32] In many ways, the group's performance at Mount Morris Park in Harlem was their coming out party. They were appearing as part of the festival's "Gospel Day" showcase, but they were playing before a huge general audience at an event that was widely known as the Soul Festival. While the film features many remarkable performances, across a wide range of musical genres and styles, The Staple Singers are one of four acts – along with Stevie Wonder, Sly and the Family Stone, and Nina Simone – that are highlighted in *Summer of Soul*.

Questlove's film glories in providing its audiences with performances that had been largely buried for nearly 50 years, but its most notable formal feature is a reflexive technique employed for a number of interviews: subjects are shown in a studio setting watching long-lost footage of the Harlem Cultural Festival on a monitor for the very first time. Cleverly, the audience is not shown the specific images these subjects are seeing; we only see how they react to this material, and these reactions range from "awestruck" to "overwhelmed." In general, however, *Summer of Soul* can be ranked among the greatest archival or largely archival music documentaries of the last 25 years – films that have used modern digital editing technologies to full, and often dizzying, effect.[33] Because of its ambition, most of the film's featured songs are just fragments, and those that are allowed to play out in full often feature a brief cut-away to a montage sequence consisting of photographs and footage that is then combined with voice-over narration or short snippets of interviews.

The two most significant appearances by The Staple Singers occur during the film's "meaty gospel passage." At 20 minutes in length, this segment of the film is its longest and, arguably, its most important. After a profile on the Edwin Hawkins Singers and their surprise crossover hit "Oh Happy Day," we can hear Tony Lawrence, the festival's M.C., announce, "Welcome to the Gospel Music Day. Gospel folks from all over the country are here today to spread the spirit. . . . Direct from Chicago to the heart of Harlem, Papa Staple [*sic*] and The Staple Singers!" Pops's guitar starts wailing, the three Staples sisters start moaning and wailing, too, and the group launches into a revamped, Stax-era version of "Help Me Jesus," the same song they'd been

Figure 4.2 The Staple Singers perform "Help Me Jesus" in *Summer of Soul*.

featured performing at the 1964 Newport Folk Festival in *Festival*. Mavis's voice-over narration begins to recount what it felt like to perform on that stage in 1969, looking out over that huge audience, seeing so many Black people "rejoicing," and getting carried away in the spirit herself. What ensues is a brief history of The Staple Singers as told by Mavis and illustrated with archival photographs and footage, including the group's beginnings in the 1940s, and Pops's roots in Mississippi, a segment that is punctuated with a clip of Pops on *The Doris Day Show* recounting how he'd bought his first guitar for five dollars at a time when he was earning three dollars a week, 50 cents a day, picking cotton on fourteen-hour shifts.

It is at this point that Questlove's strategy shifts, as he turns to a series of interviews interspersed with more footage from the Gospel Day proceedings in order to explain the larger meaning of gospel within the Black tradition: the late Greg Tate, the cultural critic and musician; the Reverend Al Sharpton, the preacher, community leader, and activist; and Charlayne Hunter-Gault, the activist and former journalist. For Tate, gospel is history, a tradition that stretches back to the earliest days of slavery, the suppression of African culture, including music, and the "conversion to Christianity." "There's something very specific about what happened in Black America," Tate comments, "where I think the only place we could be fully expressive was in music, was in these church rituals." African Americans had taken the Christian experience and "redefined it for themselves." As a result, gospel became a force that "[channeled] the emotional core of Black people." The sound of "Help Me Jesus" has persisted throughout this section of the film, and Questlove has returned to The Staple Singers performing the song onstage again and again, but here Mavis can be seen doing a trance-like shuffle step to the song throughout much of Tate's commentary. Seconds later, as Professor Herman Stevens and the Voices of Faith arrive on the scene with an ecstatic Gospel Day performance of "Heaven is Mine," Tate continues his cultural history lesson. "There's this notion of spirit possession that comes from Africa. It's part of seeking a certain kind of release and catharsis." His insight is perfectly timed to explain the wild dancing, handclapping, spinning, and trance-like behavior captured onstage, and in the audience in response. "This is an eruption of spirit," Tate continues, "to arrive at an inner peace through being totally expressively open." Tate seems to be describing Professor Herman Stevens and the Voices of Faith, but his words could just as easily describe a number of the other featured performers in this segment: from Clara Walker and the Gospel Redeemers to Mahalia Jackson to Mavis Staples. Soon afterward, Reverend Al Sharpton picks up on this notion of gospel and the pursuit of "inner peace," suggesting that it is "more than religious," gospel is therapy, one specific to "the stress and pressure of being Black in America." "We didn't go to a psychiatrist," Sharpton adds. "We didn't go lay on a couch. We didn't know anything about therapists. But we knew Mahalia Jackson!" Cue Jackson performing a typically full-throated version of "Lord, Search My Heart" to an enthusiastic audience, losing herself in the song, practically speaking in tongues. Finally, an interview with Charlayne Hunter-Gault is used to make the case that gospel is politics, that it carried the Civil Rights Movement, that it sustained it, and that it "helped generations of people confront some of the most vicious, violent acts," as the audience is shown images of Freedom Marchers en route from Selma to Montgomery in 1965, including the crossing of the infamous Edmund Pettus Bridge. The point has been made concisely yet forcefully: gospel is history, therapy, and politics. Gospel is the foundation of the African American experience, it is the crucible, and it is the balm. All of which brings us to the climax of the gospel passage.

Suddenly, the audience is thrust into a somber ceremony led by the Reverend Jesse Jackson mourning one of *the* "most vicious, violent acts," certainly one of the most devastating: the assassination of Martin Luther King Jr. Backing Rev. Jackson was the saxophonist Ben Branch and his Operation Breadbasket Orchestra, an outfit that had been created to promote King's Operation Breadbasket campaign in Chicago, which used picket lines, boycotts, and other tactics, as Sharpton explains – to get major corporations "to bring more blacks onto their payrolls," and which was spearheaded by Jackson.[34] Notably, when King launched Operation Breadbasket, Rev. Jackson was unknown in Chicago, so he reached out to his friend Pops Staples about performing on Saturdays at the organization's namesake food drives to raise awareness.[35] These concerts were a success, and soon Chicago's powerful WVON ("Voice of the Negro") radio station began airing weekly Operation Breadbasket performances featuring The Staple Singers, Ben Branch and his orchestra, and others.[36] The campaign was a coup for Rev. Jackson, creating 2,000 jobs for Blacks in its first fifteen months and providing him with a national profile.[37] It initiated a lifelong devotion to The Staple Singers, one that led to Rev. Jackson encouraging Al Bell to take on the task of producing the group himself. This connection also resulted in Stax supporting Operation Breadbasket and its successor, Operation PUSH (People United to Save Humanity), as well as Jackson getting signed to Respect, Stax's explicitly political subsidiary, in order to release a series of spoken-word albums, including *I Am Somebody* (1971), featuring the same monologue he would deliver to an audience of 100,000 at Wattstax.[38]

As Rev. Jackson explains, the central attraction of this set will be a "prayer," a performance of "Precious Lord" – Dr. King's favorite song – by Mahalia Jackson – King's favorite singer, and a close friend and political ally.[39] Adding to the gravitas of the occasion, as Rev. Jackson explains, is the fact that he and Branch were with King in Memphis the week of his assassination, that they were staying with King in the Lorraine Motel, and that King's last words, immediately before he got shot, were to Branch: a request that he and his orchestra play "Precious Lord" at that night's rally. Rev. Jackson underlines the song's politics while paraphrasing it: "He didn't die crying and

Figure 4.3 Mavis Staples and Mahalia Jackson perform "Precious Lord" in *Summer of Soul*.

dying afraid, he died asking the Lord to lead his hand, to help him lead us." The audience appears to be in deep mourning, heads bowed – especially when a clip of King's "Mountaintop" speech is played over the P.A. – but the ceremony and the therapy has just begun.

Famously, as Mavis Staples explains in voice-over, "Sister Mahalia" wasn't feeling well that day – what was typically a solo number became a duet, as Mahalia asked Mavis to help her out. Mavis takes the opening verse, and from the moment she sings the words "Precious Lord" the response of the audience is immediate ("Go ahead!" "Roll call!"), but as she continues and goes into preacher mode – jumping in place, raising and waving her hand, convulsing as she belts out the lyrics, "sanctified, not sanctimonious" – the appreciation and the applause grows.[40] Mount Morris Park has been transformed into a gospel revival and the crowd is enraptured. Rev. Jackson coaxes Mahalia into taking the microphone, and she complies and delivers mightily, utterly losing herself in the song by the end of the second verse. At which point Mavis joins her, and as Wesley Morris put it in the *Times*,

> they embark on the single most astounding duet I've ever heard, seen or felt. They share the microphone. They pass it between them. Howling, moaning, wailing, hopping, but well within the song's generous contours and, somehow, in control of themselves.[41]

Up until this moment, Questlove's treatment of the long, powerful, and poignant preamble to "Precious Lord" has been subdued but forceful, the words of Rev. Jackson and the sounds of Ben Branch and his orchestra punctuated with clips of Operation Breadbasket's rallies and actions, an interview with Jackson recounting the events of April 3 and April 4, 1968, in Memphis, footage of the Lorraine Motel and King and his entourage arriving there, and an archival photograph of the murder scene. From the moment Mavis launches into the song, however, the compositions get tighter and more intimate, and Questlove's editing never strays from the duet, its attention riveted to the building storm that is the performance, picking out meaningful details like Mavis's hand held aloft, heavenward, and accentuating the sheer, unbridled power of two legendary singers giving every ounce of themselves to the occasion.

The significance of this moment has deep roots. The song itself, "Precious Lord, Take My Hand" is a revered song in the gospel repertoire in large part because it was written by Thomas A. Dorsey, the Father of African-American Gospel Music, on the occasion of the loss of his wife and child (both of them dying in childbirth) in 1932.[42] Dorsey would go on to compose "more imaginative songs," as gospel scholar Anthony Heilbut has noted, "but the simple eloquence of 'Precious Lord' eclipsed them all."[43] The song proved pivotal for Dorsey. He'd started his career as a blues musician in Georgia, before relocating to Chicago as part of the Great Migration – like Pops Staples and countless others – where he joined Ma Rainey, "the Mother of the Blues," and her band and recorded blues sides under the stage name Georgia Tom.[44] "Precious Lord" was the song that marked his full conversion from a secular artist to a sacred one. By the late 1930s, Dorsey had connected with a young contralto named Mahalia Jackson who was also a southern transplant – in this case from New Orleans – and together they began to spread the word of Dorsey's songwriting skills and his innovative combination of Black hymns and spirituals with country blues, an approach that soon came to be known as "gospel music."[45] It should be noted, that combination – Black hymns, spirituals, and country blues – is the very essence of The Staple Singers' sound. One of the things that made their sound unique was the way it remained anchored to the country blues, albeit in an electrified and distorted Chicago fashion.

By the 1950s, "Precious Lord" was central to the gospel canon, and although the song had been recorded a number of times before, Mahalia Jackson's 1956 recording was seen by many as the definitive version.[46] The song became something of a calling card in the years that followed: performed live by Aretha Franklin in her debut recording at the age of 14; performed live by Mavis Staples and The Staple Singers as part of their *Freedom Highway* session in 1965.[47] Legend of King's final words must have spread lightning-fast, because on April 7, 1968, just three days after the murder, Nina Simone performed the song in tribute at a festival in New York.[48] And, of course, Mahalia Jackson had the dubious honor of performing "Precious Lord" at Dr. King's funeral, a rendition that was said to be profoundly moving.[49]

Through this "prayer" in Mount Morris Park – through *gospel music* – the tragedy of King's murder was, at least momentarily, redeemed. But this was more than just a revival – it was also a rally. This performance was an intervention on the part of Chicago's progressive Black Christian coalition unleashed upon Harlem. Significantly, the scene ends on an ebullient note, Ben Branch blowing his saxophone, the orchestra cutting loose, Mahalia Jackson smiling and enjoying herself, Jesse Jackson conducting, The Staples sisters clapping their hands, the audience joining in the good times, and Mavis, in voice-over, getting the final word on the topic of music as therapy: "[When] you talk about music – this Black festival. . . . It's some of every kind, some of every style – jazz, blues, gospel – all of it is good, all of it makes you *feel* good."

Conclusion

A few months after the Harlem festival, on Thanksgiving Day, The Staple Singers were playing to a difficult gospel audience in Philadelphia. Maintaining a foothold in the world of gospel while simultaneously embracing the secular world of soul and funk was a tough trick to pull off, and this Philly crowd was letting the group know exactly how they felt. In response, Pops Staples told the crowd, "Don't nobody want to go to heaven more than I do, children, but we got to live down here too" – in other words, there was much work to be done in the here and now. It is this tension that we find in *Soul* to Soul, Wattstax, and, indeed, in *Summer of Soul*. The Staple Singers represented the gospel tradition in all three of these films, but they also represented so much more – they were "more than religious," to paraphrase Rev. Sharpton. Their sound now encompassed a shift toward pop music, coupled with a shift toward a much more insistent set of political appeals: agit-pop for the Black Power era. Ultimately, what *Summer of Soul* underscores with its potent combination of hope and mourning, pain and defiance, is just how relevant and how urgent this chapter in our cultural history remains.[50] As we have seen, among its numerous breath-taking achievements, Questlove's film serves as a catalyst for a robust reexamination of a critical, and highly radicalized, period in the early history of the rockumentary, one that holds the potential to shift our understanding of the genre as a whole.

Notes

1. The voice is consistent with that of Darryl Lewis, a festival attendee who is featured prominently in the film's interviews.
2. Even a music scholar and cultural historian of Questlove's stature was apparently unaware of the Harlem Cultural Festival when he was first approached about the project. Bruce Handy, "Questlove Remembers the Black Woodstock," *The New Yorker*, July 12 & 19, 2021, www.newyorker.com/magazine/2021/07/12/questlove-remembers-the-black-woodstock.
3. As Moayeri has pointed out, the footage was not as deeply buried as the film makes it out to have been, and it had been televised. Lily Moayeri, "Actually the Revolution WAS Televised," *Book & Film Globe*, 29 July 2021, https://bookandfilmglobe.com/film/summer-of-soul-lost-footage/.
4. Wesley Morris is among those critics who called *Summer of Soul* a "concert movie." Wesley Morris, "In 1969 Harlem, a Music Festival Stuns," *The New York Times*, June 24, 2021, www.nytimes.com/2021/06/24/movies/summer-of-soul-review.html. Scholars like Baker (2014) and Iversen and MacKenzie (2021), who follow Baker's lead quite closely, have lumped all "concert and other performance-based rockumentaries" under a single sub-genre, but I see value in distinguishing between concert films, festival films, and tour films.
5. The other films in this elite group are Brigitte Berman's *Artie Shaw: Time Is All You've Got* (1985), Malik Bendjelloul's *Searching for Sugar Man* (2012), Morgan Neville's *Twenty Feet from Stardom* (2013), and Asif Kapadia's *Amy* (2015).
6. Questlove, with Ben Greenman, *Music Is History* (New York: Abrams Image, 2021), 13.
7. Morris, "In 1969 Harlem, a Festival Stuns."
8. Ibid.
9. Ron Neal, "The Black Arts Movement," *The Drama Review* 12, no. 4, Black Theatre (Summer, 1968): 28. For more on the Black Arts Movement, see Amy Abugo Ongiri, *Spectacular Blackness: The Cultural Politics of the Black Power Movement and the Search for a Black Aesthetic* (Charlottesville, VA: University of Virginia Press, 2009); and Peniel E. Joseph, *The Sword and the Shield: The Revolutionary Lives of Malcolm X and Martin Luther King Jr.* (New York: Basic Books, 2020), 196.
10. Ongiri, *Spectacular Blackness*, 24, 56.
11. On the Soul to Soul Festival as a "Black Woodstock," see David E. James, *Rock 'n' Film: Cinema's Dance with Popular Music* (New York: Oxford University Press, 2016), 336. On Wattstax as a "Black Woodstock," see James, *Rock 'n' Film*, 344,

and Donna Murch, "The Many Meanings of Watts: Black Power, *Wattstax*, and the Carceral State," *OAH Magazine of History* 26, no. 1 (2012): 37.
12. This anecdote is recounted by Mavis in voice-over in *Summer of Soul*.
13. More recently, film and music scholars have begun to rectify this situation. For a good example of a book that has taken a much more expansive approach to studying popular music films, see James, *Rock 'n' Film*.
14. James, *Rock 'n' Film*, 335–36.
15. Ibid., 335–36. Because of his successes, Nkrumah became an inspiration to civil rights leaders like Martin Luther King Jr. and Malcolm X, both of whom travelled to Ghana to visit this anti-colonial icon in person, as well as to the Black Arts Movement. For the influence of Nkrumah, see Joseph, *The Sword and the Shield* and Neal, "The Black Arts Movement," 28.
16. James, *Rock 'n' Film*, 335–36.
17. Ibid., 336.
18. Ibid.
19. Robert Darden, *Nothing But Love in God's Water, Vol. 2* (University Park: The Pennsylvania State University Press, 2016), 3.
20. Liner notes, *Soul to Soul: Music from the Original Soundtrack*, Atlantic Records, 1971, vinyl LP.
21. Gavin Petrie, *Black Music* (London, New York, Sydney, and Toronto: Hamlyn Publishing Group, Ltd., 1974), 22; Rob Bowman, *Soulsville, USA: The Story of Stax Records* (New York: Schirmer Books, 1997), 211.
22. Bowman, *Soulsville, USA*, 210; Greg Kot, *I'll Take You There: Mavis Staples, The Staple Singers, and the March Up Freedom's Highway* (New York, London, Toronto, Sydney, and New Delhi: Scribner, 2014), 159.
23. Bowman, *Soulsville, USA*, 268.
24. James, *Rock 'n' Film*, 339.
25. Ibid.
26. Wolper would go on to produce *Roots* (1977), the television miniseries based on the novel by Alex Haley that was the inspiration for the name of Questlove's hip hop group the Roots.
27. James, *Rock 'n' Film*, 339–40.
28. Ibid., 339.
29. Bowman, *Soulsville, USA*, 268.
30. Kot, *I'll Take You There*, 195.
31. Bowman, *Soulsville, USA*, 270.
32. Moayeri, "Actually the Revolution WAS Televised."
33. Some of the films that come to mind in this regard are Julien Temple's *The Filth and the Fury* (2000), Todd Haynes's *The Velvet Underground* (2021), and Brett Morgen's *Moonage Daydream* (2022).
34. Kot, *I'll Take You There*, 113.
35. Ibid.
36. Ibid.
37. The figure of 50,000 jobs appears in the Bowman book. Elsewhere in my notes, I saw that Kot stated that 2,000 jobs had been created. This figure (2,000 jobs) is the same figure I'm finding elsewhere in my research (e.g., https://kinginstitute.stanford.edu/operation-breadbasket).
38. James, *Rock 'n' Film*, 338; Bowman, *Soulsville, USA*, 202.
39. Anthony Heilbut, *The Gospel Sound: Good News and Bad Times* (New York: Limelight Editions, 1985), 70–71.
40. Remnick, David, "The Gospel According to Mavis Staples," *The New Yorker*, July 4, 2022.
41. Morris, "In 1969, a Music Festival Stuns."

42. Mark, Burford, "Family Affairs, Part II: Black Baptists and Chicago Gospel," *Mahalia Jackson and the Black Gospel Field* (New York: Oxford Academic, 2018), accessed October 31, 2022, https://doi-org.proxy.library.brocku.ca/10.1093/oso/9780190634902.003.0003; Darden Notes, "Even Today, 'Take My Hand, Precious Lord,' Is Heard at Virtually Every African-American Funeral in the United States." Darden, *Nothing But Love in God's Water*, Vol. 2, 5.
43. Heilbut, *The Gospel Sound*, 31.
44. Judith Tick, ed., with Paul Beaudoin, "Thomas Andrew Dorsey 'Brings the People Up' and Carries Himself Along," in *Music in the USA: A Documentary Companion* (New York: Oxford University Press, 2008), 404.
45. Robert Darden, *Nothing But Love in God's Water, Vol. 1* (University Park: The Pennsylvania State University Press, 2014), 90.
46. Kot, *I'll Take You There*, 145.
47. Jerry Wexler, "'Handcrafting the Grooves' in the Studio: Aretha Franklin at Muscle Shoals," in *Music in the USA: A Documentary Companion*, eds. Judith Tick, with Paul Beaudoin (New York: Oxford University Press, 2008), 614.
48. Darden, *People Get Ready!*, 10. Darden states that Simone performed the song "two days" after King's assassination, but, in fact, she performed the song on April 7, 1968, three days after the tragedy (www.ninasimone.com/1960-1969/legacy-1968/).
49. Aretha Franklin, in turn, had the dubious honor of performing "Precious Lord" at Mahalia Jackson's funeral in Chicago in January 1972, just two weeks after she had re-recorded the song live in Los Angeles for her extraordinary *Amazing Grace* sessions. These performances at the New Temple Missionary Baptist Church were the subject of another lost film, *Amazing Grace*, which was shot by Sydney Pollack in 1972, but only saw the light of day in 2018, after Franklin's death and after the material had been re-edited by Alan Elliott.
50. Here, I'm paraphrasing Rev. Sharpton from the film, discussing Nina Simone and her ability to express the contradictions of the Black community. As I'm suggesting, his words capture a fundamental tension in *Summer of Soul*.

5 "Music in the Air"
Spirituality and Revival in *Summer of Soul*

Michele Prettyman

The title of this chapter references the powerful gospel song "Up Above My Head I Hear Music in the Air" written by Sister Rosetta Tharpe. Tharpe was introduced as "the great spiritual singer" before a 1965 performance in France and was a musical innovator and a pioneer of gospel and rock and roll.[1] Dubbing her a "spiritual singer" is no small thing as it recognizes the expansive power in her writing and her performance.[2] Tharpe's words provide a roadmap connecting black musical performance to powerful modes of spiritual experience. The song's lyrics "Up above my head I hear music in the air" and "I really do believe there's a Heaven somewhere" capture music's capacity to live in an ethereal "somewhere" and also in the confines of human experience, channeling hearing into *believing*.[3]

The song's ethereal language frames my discussion of black concert films and spirituality, specifically Ahmir "Questlove" Thompson's *Summer of Soul: (. . . Or, When the Revolution Could Not Be Televised)* (2021), which brings the recently discovered footage of the Harlem Cultural Festival back to life. Released 50 years after the concerts took place, the film weaves musical performances with contemporary interviews of performers and concertgoers illuminating the cultural zeitgeist of Harlem and much of Black America of the time.

The Spirit of the Black Concert Film

While Daphne Brooks and Gina Arnold have previously written about the Harlem Cultural Festival, *Summer of Soul* invites a reimagining of the concert festival film and reveals deep ties, not just to the black performance archive, but to traditions of black gathering and spiritual sociality.[4] And while Barbara Ehrenreich in her book *Dancing in the Streets* makes the case that many forms of 'ecstatic' social gathering and festivals (including rock concerts and festivals) across many cultures are often "united in joy and exaltation," I make the case that *Summer of Soul* captures a precise connection to black revivalism, one rooted in a spiritual, liberatory set of experiences.[5]

Before discussing spirituality, revival, and performance, which form the next sections of this chapter, I want to first provide some brief context for a set of black concert films around the time of the Harlem Cultural Festival. Two of these films take place in Africa: *Soul to Soul* (Denis Sanders, 1971), which documents the Soul to Soul Independence Day Festival in Ghana in 1971, and *Soul Power* (Jeff Levy-Hinte, 2009), which chronicles the music festival attached to the 1974 boxing match between Muhammad Ali and George Foreman in Kinshasa, Zaire (now the Democratic Republic of the Congo). These concert films feature African American performers like Wilson Pickett, Ike and Tina Turner, Les McCann and Eddie Harris, The Staple Singers, Roberta Flack and the Voices of East Harlem (in *Soul to Soul*) and James Brown, B.B. King, and The Spinners (in *Soul Power*).[6] These performers were certainly popular global figures, commercially successful, and likely to draw crowds in their respective locations, but they were also powerful exemplars of a black cultural hermeneutic which offered African countries in varying stages of anti-colonial liberation a glimpse of black power in a compelling context. Many of these artists had risen from rural and urban poverty to use their artistry to give voice to a wide range of concerns while challenging the American cultural status quo. Characterizing their impact, Emily Lordi explains:

> Above all, insofar as soul artists working in the 1960s and 70s were navigating a sociopolitical landscape that resembles our own – in its spectacular anti-black violence as well as its radical mobilization – the soul revival reflects an effort to reclaim soul artists as models of expressing black resistance, joy, and togetherness through the medium of popular song.[7]

However, *Summer of Soul* more explicitly aligns with another subset of black concert documentary films that actualize a spirit of self-possession, ecstatic release, and transformation amid a turbulent socio-political environment. The first and most well-known, *Wattstax* (Mel Stuart, 1972), takes place in Los Angeles and features colorful and seemingly uncensored community dialogue. Including conversations on sex, love, and religion and the unfiltered commentary of Richard Pryor, the film's taglines describe it as "The Soulful Expression of the Black Experience" and "The Living Word." Of particular interest is how *Wattstax* captures community members' commentary on religious "shouting" and its extensive montage of black churches intercut with a gut-wrenching performance of James Cleveland's gospel standard "Peace Be Still" by The Emotions. Other films in this archive focus on gospel music including *Amazing Grace* (Alan Elliott and Sydney Pollack, 2018), which features two days of dynamic performances by Aretha Franklin at the New Temple Missionary Baptist Church (James Cleveland's church in Los Angeles) in 1972, and *Say Amen, Somebody* (George Nierenberg, 1982), which follows the lives of gospel singers Willie Mae Ford Smith and Thomas Dorsey and features an extensive concert sequence at the end of the film. These concert films emphasize the power of black spiritual gathering and sociality as a force that lives long after the concert or film viewing experience is over, and this is evidenced in *Summer of Soul* in the poignant interview recollections of those who attended the concerts nearly 50 years later.

While *Summer of Soul* does not focus solely on gospel music, I argue that powerful elements of spirituality influence the performers, their performances, and the concert space/staging and are reinforced in the making of the film. These elements include

- a vibrant outdoor atmosphere (as opposed to the confines of a church, concert hall, or some other enclosure);
- an inclination toward personal and collective revival and transformation;
- a powerful symbiotic relationship between performers and the audience, which I describe as an 'encounter'; and
- experiences of release and transfiguration alternately known as "shouting," "getting happy," or "catching the spirit."

I discuss how these elements surface throughout the film, emphasizing two particular styles of spiritual performance: new age and gospel. Ultimately, *Summer of Soul* reconstructs individual and collective memory while illuminating how audiences and performers might be moved and might move us in profound ways. The film and the people in them are not simply part of a cultural archive but are a spiritual force summoning us to experience the possibilities of renewal and transformation.

Spirituality and Musical Performance

Ethnomusicologist Franya Berkman aptly notes that in the secular academy "spirituality has taken a back seat to the so-called important stories of political history."[8] Yet there is a gathering interest in imagining new trajectories and parameters to explore spirituality often using the analytics of being, consciousness, soul, cosmology, metaphysics, and liberatory praxis. This work flows across theological, performative, feminist, cultural, and black studies, not to mention the field of Africana Esoteric Studies (AES).[9] Without space for a full review of the literature, it is important to consider the work of important scholars who articulate some of the capacities and possibilities of spiritual discourse as it relates to black musical performance. For instance, Emmett G. Price III writes that "spirituality and music were (and remain) important tools in Black America's quest for freedom."[10] He explains that "In many ways, it is the presence of spiritual influences or spirituality within the music, observed in the spirituals, blues, and other forms of black music, which allows for the possibility of the transition from survival to liberation."[11] Finally for Price, "The spiritual ethos in black music is the reviving force that flows from generation through generation exposing traditions, exploiting legacies, and constantly illuminating heritage to make known the repetitive cycle of life that comes from beyond."[12] This context makes important connections between music and spirituality, yet I want to provide more context for spirituality explicitly.

While drawing on Price, I also lean heavily on the work of Akasha Gloria Hull, whose work on spirituality emerged from her studies of black women writers and intensive research into their literary, writerly, and spiritual practices. Hull provides a useful point of departure, as she writes:

> Spirituality, as I view it, involves a conscious relationship with the realism of spirit, with the invisibly permeating, ultimately positive, divine, and evolutionary energies that give rise to and sustain all that exists . . . this spiritual expression builds on firm cultural foundations and traditional Christian religions, but also freely incorporates elements popularly called "New Age" . . . Eastern philosophies of cosmic connectedness and others.[13]

Hull's framework is both expansive and precise, accounting for the myriad ways in which black life engages spiritual and religious practice. In a related vein, I also rely on the work of Gayle Wald and Emily Lordi who articulate, often through discourses on "soul," and "vibrations," how a performative "spirit" lives in the cultural and expressive performance and practices of black people.[14] Wald notes how

> soul bridged the sacred-secular divide. In both Christian and Muslim religious traditions, it referred to an inviolable essence that linked individuals to the Almighty, whereas in a worldly context it named a commercially and critically ascendent black cultural style of the 1960s.[15]

Likewise, Lordi explains that "the 1960s soul came to signify the special resilience black people had earned by surviving the historical and daily trials of white supremacy. At a moment when it was becoming possible to describe oneself as 'spiritual but not religious.'"[16]

Finally, I find powerful evidence of an awareness of spiritual experience grounded in black musical performance in the language of Paul Gilroy, who writes of Jimi Hendrix's phrase "the electric church," which Gilroy describes as

> a collective social body of musical celebrants that gathered periodically to engage the amplified modernist offshoots of the Mississippi delta and harness them in the causes of human creativity and liberation. Its ritual events had become loud, he told Dick Cavett in July 1969, not only because the appalling state of the world meant that many people were in need of being woken up by the shock that elevated volume could supply, but also because if the wake-up-call could only be delivered on the correct

frequency it could, in turn, promote a direct encounter with the souls of the people involved.[17]

Gilroy surmises:

> Music would now produce its own public world: a social corona that could nourish or host an alternative sensibility [sic] a structure of feeling that might function to make wrongs and injustices more bearable in the short term but could also promote a sense of different possibilities, provide healing glimpses of an alternative moral, artistic, and political order.[18]

While Gilroy does not use the term "spiritual" and, through Hendrix, applies pressure to an explicitly religious framework, we use some shared language around how sonic, musical, and communal frequencies "take us higher," transforming the world around us. Gilroy and the other scholars cited here emphasize the importance of feeling, healing, and the desire for a collective awakening and renewal – vital elements of a spiritual praxis which are captured in *Summer of Soul*. Thus, spirituality here is not beholden to a set of specific ideologies or belief systems but an open invitation to explore, experience, commune, and create with a renewed sense of possibilities.

Revive Us Again

Essential to this spiritual paradigm is the notion of revival.[19] Traditionally, American religious revivals are outdoor church services often held under tents during the summer months, where attendees bear witness to the pleasures of "music in the air" and fellowship outdoors without confinement in churches or concert halls. Some attending the service might be stirred or moved to the point of physical, emotional, or internal transfiguration. While typically framed in an explicitly religious context, I frame revival as a kind of spiritual experience not wedded to the histories of the Great and Second Awakenings or through the Reconstruction era of American history. However, consider David Blight's compelling description of revival in a more evangelical context:

> This was not a distant, far-away God in some kind of institutional church, but it was a God, said the evangelicals, involved in the daily lives of people, involved in every thought and every deed of your life. . . . There had never been anything like it. Here's a meeting of 3,000 people out in a field, blacks and whites together, listening to a preacher who says, "Here in my message is a new life for you, here's a new chance for you. Here's a God who had your interest at heart. Here's a God who may deliver you."[20]

Blight's account of revival speaks to a collective and dynamic human catharsis and a shared pursuit of transformation. I use the term "revival" to emphasize an unencumbered openness yielding to the naturalistic environment and the free movement of these extant energies through musical performance.[21] Like spirituality, the notion of revival is not confined to a particular history of religious ritual but rather characterized as an openness to transformational praxes at the intersections of sacred, secular, and out-of-body experiences. The notion of revival is not solely a "black" phenomenon, yet it exists within a panoply of forms of gathering held sacred in historical and contemporary communities of black people, including the ring shout, singing, and praying bands, and camp meetings.[22]

Central to my discussion of spirituality is the notion of "encounter," which I use to describe how we are moved, transfixed, awed, and changed by one another. Extending far beyond an appreciation of talent, musicianship, virtuosity, beauty, or celebrity, *Summer of Soul* shifts the dynamic between concertgoer, performer, and film viewer from simply watching a concert or concert film to witnessing and participating in a transformative encounter.[23] Lordi expounds on the relationship between performers and audiences of this era, saying, "Much of the music gathered under the capacious banner in the 1960s carried elements of gospel music onto a secular stage, channeling a revival-style performative energy."[24] She also provides a way of thinking about revival through the performance of soul artists like Sly Stone (discussed later). She writes: "Everything seemed to be petering out when the song suddenly revives. We might hear in this false ending an enactment of soul resilience –a refusal to die down, a refusal to end."[25] Lordi's "false ending" is a structural and symbolic act of revival as it refers to "the act of bringing a song to a close and then striking it back up again."[26] These structural performative nuances resonate throughout *Summer of Soul*, reminding us that when all hope seems to have gone, we can be summoned, revived, and – like the footage of the Harlem Cultural Festival – brought back to life.

New Age Performance and Connection

In *Summer of Soul*, two styles of performance release powerful spiritual energy and connection to audiences. Both styles evoke and channel the aforementioned dimensions of encounter and transformation, but they each rely on particular dynamics to move the crowd. The first style I refer to as "new age" performance, which includes those of The 5th Dimension and Sly and the Family Stone. I use the term "new age" in a few ways. First, it aligns with the curiosity and interest in the "Age of Aquarius" spiritual discourse prevalent in the 1960s, a sensibility that was popular among many African Americans. Akasha Gloria Hull explains that "black spiritual expression builds on firm cultural foundations and traditional Christian religions but also freely incorporates elements popularly called 'New Age' – Tarot, chakra work, psychic enhancement, numerology, Eastern philosophies of cosmic connectedness, and others."[27] Hull also cites the definition of "new age" given by Toni Cade Bambara as "everybody's ancient wisdom," referring to "very old systems of spiritual attunement that appear in slightly differing forms but with the same essential content in all root cultures."[28] I also use "new age" to account for principles and practices that transgress gender, sexual, and social norms and the boundaries between secular and sacred spheres, while also valorizing principles like connection, harmony, balance, and unity.

The 5th Dimension takes full advantage of the concert's staging, which collapses the distance between audience and performer, positioning the audience in physical and emotional proximity to the stage where performers are able to dance and shake hands with audience members. Breaking down barriers between the audience and performers empowers the crowd and creates a sense of harmony between them. This connection is affirmed in the present-day footage of Marilyn McCoo and Billy Davis Jr. of The 5th Dimension, who are transfixed by the images and memories that come flooding back to them. McCoo tearfully reveals in her interview that "We were so happy to be there . . . we wanted our people to know what we were about, and we were hoping that they would receive us." Adrienne Pryor of the gospel group the Edwin Hawkins Singers similarly describes being moved by watching footage of the crowds saying, "My first reaction was . . . my God." Mavis Staples evokes a similar sense of awe in her comments, as she says, "When I looked out onto the crowd, I was overtaken with joy. I just saw so many black people and they were rejoicing, and they were having a good time and I started celebrating with them."

The 5th Dimension, exemplars of a spiritually grounded "new age" ethos, connects black musical traditions and the spiritual zeitgeist of the time. Their amalgamation of influences is evident in their lyrics, album covers, and onstage performances. The first song they perform in *Summer of Soul*, "Don't Ya Hear Me Callin to Ya," mixes a funky, psychedelic sound with gospel and folk harmonies designed to reach the musically savvy Harlem audience. The song literally calls to the audience, "Can you hear me calling to ya," entreating the audience and the group to come together, as Davis's lead vocal refrain repeats, "come on home" reflecting the band's longing for a shared sense of community. The song itself assuages the group's concerns about how they were often described as a "black group with a white sound," voicing their desire to be felt, heard, and understood by a black Harlem audience. They wanted to be seen as "kids from St. Louis, Missouri" who, as McCoo explains, "wanted to sing R & B, pop, and we wanted to have a jazz influence." This song is intercut with a photograph of the group jumping in the air in London and the cover of their album "Up Up and Away" featuring the words "Go Where You Want to Go" along with an image of the group in the signature hot-air balloon. These images and text, along with the group's name, upbeat energy, and sound, embody an aesthetic of freedom, ascendancy, or elevation to another dimension.

The second song they performed, "Age of Aquarius/Let the Sunshine In," was the number one song on the pop charts in 1969 and the group's best-known song. Originally performed in the countercultural theatrical hit *Hair*, the song embodies the spiritual aspirations of the era's turbulent social history. The song's lyrics, which include words like "harmony and understanding," "mystic crystal revelation," and "the mind's true liberation," emphasize essential elements of 1960s spiritual discourse, and they are sung with vigor and passion by the group. Later the group sings "When you feel like you've been mistreated, just open your heart" capturing the essence of new-age mysticism and speaking to the legacies of racialized trauma experienced by communities of black people in Harlem and the country. Onstage, the group slows the pace, waving their arms and moving their bodies in a homogenized, synchronized fashion, almost like tai chi. They flow across the stage wearing the same style of outfit in bright orange, yellow, and brown – clothing that de-emphasizes gender, body type, and any physical differences between group members. Dancing with members of the audience, Davis, who sang gospel in his youth explains, "We travel all over the world, and our main purpose in traveling is just to bring and spread a little love." While these values and aesthetics were more often attributed to hippies and the countercultural movement and framed as "white," McCoo asks, "How do you color a sound?" The 5th Dimension performance makes the case that these values emanate from shared sensibilities rooted in both a black spiritual ethos *and* a cosmic human framework. The group's performance breaks down walls between audience/performer and between raced bodies and styles of music. More importantly, it embodies an ethos of equality, openness, and the power of an expansive spirituality and suggests that black performative and spiritual life persist in spite of restrictions and trauma.

Sly and the Family Stone are the final act in the film and further exemplify new-age performance. Their set is placed just after a sequence of black-and-white images from the film, which depict the aftermath of the concerts and the subsequent discarding or erasure of their history. The images show the site of the festival emptied of people and the grounds littered with debris, intercut with frames of stacks of footage of the festival that were left to rot for 50 years. In voice-over, Stevie Wonder decries that the powers that be didn't see the footage as significant enough to "keep it as a part of history," followed by Gladys Knight, who states, "We as a people, especially today, need to feel like family, holding up for each other, fighting for each other, lifting each other up." Then the voice of Sly Stone is heard, as he feels out the crowd, "We're going try to sing a song together if we can now. The song is called 'Higher,' and we want everybody to join in. Don't wait for approval from your neighbor because your neighbor might be waiting for you." Soon he exclaims, "Wanna take you higher," raising his arm in a unifying and defiant gesture as the audience respond in a thunderous collective voice with their arms raised, chanting "Higher!" and ushering in the boisterous and earth-shaking final performance in the film.

Sly and his band of siblings – male and female, black and white – rock, reel, and stomp across the stage. Sly and his actual sister Rose, famous for donning a platinum wig, dance and move in a way that reflects their upbringing. Emily Lordi explains that "They honed their prodigious skills at a Church of God in Christ in San Francisco where they sang with their family gospel quartet the Stewart Four."[29] And while the band's composition and style appeared to bend toward a racial and gender egalitarianism and a liberatory performative style, Lordi describes a tendency in Sly to produce a "domineering performance that should temper idealized visions of the mixed-race, mixed-gender band as a utopic familial network."[30] It is this "utopic" tension that for me lies at the heart of the spiritual taxonomy of the black concert film. These performances and the ethos and values that are demonstrated, professed, or encountered at a spiritual level do not simply transcend the very real lived experiences of the audiences, viewers, or performers. But it is the desire – amid trauma, pain, anxiety, conflict, and loss – to tap into a collective need for transfiguration, to be remade, reborn, renewed, and revived through music, performance, and black gathering that is affirmed, and that transcends a specific performer or a moment in time. Sly and the Family Stone's admonition to be taken "Higher" is the hope of accessing another dimension of individual and collective awareness and new age, cosmic elevation; it is the possibility of coexisting, in spite of all attempts to debilitate, demoralize, and disconnect us.

"Catching the Spirit" Through Gospel Performance

In his interview in the film, the late, great musician and cultural critic Greg Tate discusses gospel performances and their impact on generations of black people. Tate explains:

> There's something very specific about Black America where I think that the only place, we could be fully expressive, was in music, was in these church rituals. Gospel was channeling the emotional core of Black people who were insiders as Christians. They experienced it and redefined it for themselves and that goes all the way back, probably, to the first moments of Black conversion to Christianity.

Tate's insights are intercut with footage of black parishioners in church settings who are "catching the spirit," then back to concert footage of Prof.

Herman Stevens and the Voices of Faith who move across the stage and shout. As film viewers watch the folks on stage and in the crowd, "catching the spirit," Tate's voice resumes, saying,

> there is this notion of spirit possession from Africa, it's a part of seeking a certain kind of release and catharsis. . . . This is an eruption of spirit. To arrive at an inner peace by being completely, expressively open.

Civil rights activist Charlayne Hunter-Gault follows Tate in the film, explaining that "gospel is in our DNA, it's deep in the recesses of my consciousness."

The second musical style, exemplified by Mavis Staples, Pops Staples and The Staple Singers, Mahalia Jackson and the powerful duet featuring Jackson and Mavis Staples, is rooted in the gospel tradition, yet I argue that it exceeds the parameters of traditional gospel performance. As "music in the air," these performances elicit strong reactions from many in the crowd enacting a powerful sense of release, and as the film documents, this release reverberates in the atmosphere, in the spiritual lives of the performers and audiences, and across American cultural history. This release is often referred to as "catching the spirit," and it accounts for modes of ecstatic and joyful release, expressive movement, connection to a Divine entity or spirit possession.[31] The sequence of gospel music performance is anchored by Mavis Staples, and her family, and her recollections of performing at the Harlem Cultural Festival form a bridge that unites viewers and performers to traditions of black musical performance and to an experience of spiritual connection.

Figure 5.1 An image of Mavis Staples superimposed over the crowd emphasizes the ethereal oneness between performer and audience.

Staples's voice-over in the film states:

> In 1969 we were singing gospel, but we would be invited to folk festivals, jazz festivals, blues festivals . . . I said to Daddy–Daddy why these people inviting us to blues festivals–we don't sing no blues? He said, Mavis, listen to our music, you will hear every kind of music in our songs. In fact, it was years before my sisters, and I knew Pops was playing the blues on his guitar while we were singing gospel.

Staples' account explains the powerful musical connection between gospel, blues, folk, rock, and jazz, and it crystallizes how the power of musical performance travels beyond the artificial boundaries of form, genre, venue, style, region, or even performer.

Staples' insightful commentary is overlaid with images of the group performing "Help Me, Jesus." But before the performance, Pops Staples begins with a prayer or an incantation, saying, "Sitting around on the mourner's bench I heard an old lady in the Amen Corner, and she began to pray, and she began to moan," to which the three Staples sisters in booming voices respond with a shout, "Yaaaaaasssss!" Mavis Staples follows, "In my soul . . . I've got to move!" The Staples sisters (Mavis, Cleotha, and Yvonne), dressed in delicate, white lace dresses, stockings, and shoes, launch into the song, clapping hands and tapping their feet in choreographed unison as Pops Staples plays guitar. Their fierce harmonies and their strong raspy voices sing, "Help me, Lord Jesus, give me more faith, I need your power, help me to run this race. Help me Jesus (repeated)." The song continues, intercut with closeup reaction shots of the audience, singing, clapping, rocking from side to side, moving. Low-angle shots of Mavis Staples' mouth emphasize how the words come forcefully from her body, bursting into the atmosphere. She moves around the stage, encouraging the crowd to clap, "Let me hear you clap your hands, wonder do you feel alright" as her voice and the guitar go around on a loop, repeating these admonitions.

Gospel legend Mahalia Jackson's performance provides a powerful climactic moment of revival and release in the film. Jackson was previously featured in Bert Stern and Aram Avakian's concert film about the 1958 Newport Jazz Festival, *Jazz on a Summer's Day* (1959), but here she is captured in her full splendor. Dressed in a vibrant pink gown, matching her long-time accompanist Mildred Falls, Jesse Jackson invites Jackson and Mavis Staples back onstage to do a "prayer," that is, to sing "Precious Lord," a song that Jackson describes as "so meaningful to us" in part because it was Dr. King's favorite. As Jesse Jackson speaks, describing the last moments of King's life, the tone shifts to one of deep collective mourning. Jackson details the moments leading up to King's assassination and then describes the severing of his spinal column and that his face was "blown off." Jackson's painful recollections of King's gruesome death opens the way for a kind of catharsis, a space where the clouds of death, violence, and racial brutality can be released through the healing and power of Jackson's voice and presence. In voice-over, Mavis Staples adds another layer of context for the moment just prior to Jackson's performance as she explains, "When it came time for her to sing, she leaned over and told me, 'Baby, Hailey don't feel too good today. I need you to help me sing this song. And I said, yes ma'am. I'll help you.'"

As Mahalia Jackson utters her first notes, Jesse Jackson, who just described King's brutal death, reacts immediately, stirred to a knowing smile and a clap of the hands. He knows what's coming. As Mahalia's voice gets stronger, she too feels revived, gaining strength after confessing that her body was faltering. Her voice, the music, and the sensibilities it arouses are familiar to Jesse and to many in the crowd. Mahalia proceeds to sing with fervor and ferocity, as if she is singing for dear life. She channels, in the midst of her own physical limitations (she is suffering from a number of physical ailments at this point in her life), a gut-wrenching performance transforming the song into a vibrating, spiritual experience. Captured in medium closeups, the shots emphasize the strain of every muscle and the trembling of her face and lips. Staples joins her, and the two go back and forth, wrenching every ounce of strength between them as Jesse Jackson jumps up and down in the background. The film emphasizes low-angle shots of the women, capturing their strained expressions, their upward glances, and gestures of them raising their hands or reverently closing their eyes. Their faces are superimposed over the audience suggesting that there is a shared sensibility that conjoins them or hovers between them. Jesse Jackson and viewers experience the sheer force of the performance and the collective bond of being moved, lifted, and revived.

Summer of Soul brings back to life the expressive power of the Harlem Cultural Festival, which preceded several black music festivals in the 1970s which would become concert films. The film brings to life extant footage of musical performance with pieces of collective memory inviting viewers to bear witness to and also participate in the process of releasing a spiritual energy into the atmosphere. I emphasize spirituality as a seminal framework which is embodied in the film's emphasis on the outdoors, the energy of the crowd, the connection between audience and performer, the staging of the performances themselves, and the new age and gospel styles of music and performance. Together these dynamics reimagine the tradition of "revival," which in this context creates the conditions for a release of spiritual longing, and ultimately, modes of awareness and transformation. *Summer of Soul* literally "sets the stage" for the expression and release of an ethereal or Divine presence as viewers are summoned, moved, and stirred by the possibilities of individual and collective renewal.

Notes

1. Sister Rosetta Tharpe - Up Above My Head (France 1965)," *YouTube*, October 15, 2014, www.youtube.com/watch?v=P9BFVeZr5Sc.

2. Gayle Wald has produced an archive of work on Tharpe including a biography in which she describes Tharpe, a child performer, as "pint-sized 'singing and guitar playing miracle." See Wald, *Shout, Sister, Shout! The Untold Story of Rock-and-Roll Trailblazer Sister Rosetta Tharpe* (Boston, MA: Beacon Press, 2007), 21.
3. Ashon Crawley's description of the relationship between spirit, breath, and air is particularly relevant. See Crawley, *Blackpentecostal Breath: The Aesthetics of Possibility* (New York: Fordham University Press, 2017).
4. Daphne A. Brooks, "At 'Black Woodstock,' an All-Star Lineup Delivered Joy and Renewal to 300,000," *The New York Times*, August 15, 2019, www.nytimes.com/2019/08/15/arts/music/black-woodstock-harlem-festival-1969.html. See also Gina Arnold's important essay "'As Real as Real Can Get': Race, Representation and Rhetoric at Wattstax, 1972."
5. Barbara Ehrenreich, *Dancing in the Streets: A History of Collective Joy* (London: Granta, 2008).
6. For more on *Soul to Soul* at "AFI Catalog Spotlight: Soul to Soul," *American Film Institute*, June 30, 2023, www.afi.com/news/afi-catalog-spotlight-soul-to-soul/; on *Soul Power*, see Sean O'Hagan, "Soul Power," *The Guardian*, July 11, 2009, www.theguardian.com/film/2009/jul/12/soul-power-james-brown.
7. Lordi, *The Meaning of Soul*, 151.
8. Franya J. Berkman, *Monument Eternal: The Music of Alice Coltrane* (Middletown, CT: Wesleyan University Press, 2010), 14.
9. See the introduction "Africana Esoteric Studies: Mapping a New Endeavor," in *Esotericism in African American Religious Experience: "There Is a Mystery"...*, eds. Stephen C. Finley, Margarita Simon Guillory, and Hugh R. Page Jr. (Brill, 2014) and Marques Redd, "Those Mysteries, Our Mysteries: Ishmael Reed and the Construction of a Black Esoteric Tradition," 277–94 in the same volume.
10. See Emmett G. Price III, "The Spiritual Ethos in Black Music and Its Quintessential Exemplar, John Coltrane," in *John Coltrane and Black America's Quest for Freedom: Spirituality and the Music*, ed. Leonard L. Brown (Oxford: Oxford University Press, 2010), 155.
11. Ibid.
12. Ibid., 170.
13. Gloria T. Hull, *Soul Talk: The New Spirituality of African-American Women* (Rochester, VT: Inner Traditions, 2001), 2.
14. See Gayle Wald's discussion of vibrations in "Soul Vibrations: Black Music and Black Freedom in Sound and Space," *American Quarterly* 63, no. 3 (2011): 673–96, https://doi.org/10.1353/aq.2011.0048.
15. Gayle Wald and Chester Higgins, *It's Been Beautiful: Soul! and Black Power Television* (Durham, NC: Duke University Press, 2015), 64.
16. Lordi, *The Meaning of Soul*, 5.
17. Paul Gilroy, "Between the Blues and the Blues Dance: Some Soundscapes of the Black Atlantic," in *The Auditory Culture Reader*, eds. Michael Bull and Les Back (Berg, 2003), 383.
18. Ibid.
19. This phrasing is taken from a 19th-century hymn "Revive Us Again" written by Dr. William Mackay and often sung in black churches. I use it with some irony to also reference Common's powerful song with Stevie Wonder, "Black America Again."
20. David Blight's perspective can be found in "Africans in America | Part 2 | Religion and Slavery," *PBS*, accessed July 4, 2023, www.pbs.org/wgbh/aia/part2/2narr2.html.
21. See Sarah Jane Cervenak and J. Kameron Carter's introduction to "The Black Outdoors: Fred Moten & Saidiya Hartman," accessed July 4, 2023, https://fhi.duke.edu/videos/black-outdoors-fred-moten-saidiya-hartman.

22. For more on "singing and praying bands," see the works of Clifford Murphy at Folkways, "The Singing and Praying Bands of Maryland and Delaware: Smithsonian Folkways agazine," *Smithsonian Folkways Recordings*, accessed July 4, 2023, https://folkways.si.edu/magazine-fall-winter-2014-singing-praying-bands-maryland-delaware/gospel-african-american-sacred/music/article/smithsonian.
23. My thinking about revival is informed by Ashon Crawley, who writes in *Blackpentecostal Breath* that, "Black Study Is a Methodological Mode of Intense, Spiritual, Communal, Intellectual, Practice and Meditative Performance," 8.
24. Lordi, *The Meaning of Soul*, 20.
25. Ibid., 81.
26. Ibid., 126.
27. Hull, *Soul Talk*, 2.
28. Ibid., 3.
29. Lordi, *The Meaning of Soul*, 77.
30. Ibid.
31. I discuss this phenomenon of ecstatic release in "Flash(es) of the Spirit: Images of Black Life as a Spiritual Encounter," *World Records* 3 (2020), and Crawley takes up this explicitly in *Blackpentecostal Breath*.

Bibliography

AFI Catalog. "Spotlight: Soul to Soul." *American Film Institute*, June 30, 2023. https://www.afi.com/news/afi-catalog-spotlight-soul-to-soul/.

Akomfrah, John. "Digitopia and the Spectres of Diaspora." *Journal of Media Practice* 11, no. 1 (January 2014).

Arnold, Gina. "'As Real as Real Can Get': Race, Representation and Rhetoric at Wattstax, 1972." In *The Pop Festival: History, Music, Media, Culture*, ed. George McKay, 61–73. Bloomsbury Academic, 2015.

Auslander, Philip. *Liveness: Performance in a Mediatized Culture*, 3rd ed. London and New York: Routledge, 2023.

Bailey, Jason. "A Brief History of Violence in American Movie Theaters." *Flavorwire*, July 24, 2015. https://www.flavorwire.com/529710/a-brief-history-of-violence-in-american-movie-theaters.

Baker, Michael Brendan. "Notes on the Rockumentary Renaissance." *Cinephile* 10, no. 1 (Summer 2014).

Battaglio, Stephen. "Meet the Archivist Who Saved the Historic Footage That Became *Summer of Soul*." *Los Angeles Times*, August 19, 2021. https://www.latimes.com/entertainment-arts/business/story/2021-08-19/meet-the-archivist-who-rescued-the-concert-footage-that-became-the-summer-of-soul.

Beattie, Keith. "It's Not Only Rock and Roll: 'Rockumentary,' Direct Cinema, and Performative Display." *Australasian Journal of American Studies* 24, no. 2 (December 2005): 21–41.

———. *D.A. Pennebaker*. Champaign, IL: University of Illinois Press, 2011.

Bell, Dale. *Woodstock: An Inside Look at the Movie That Shook Up the World and Defined a Generation*. Studio City, CA: Michael Wiese Productions, 1999.

Benjamin, Walter. *The Arcades Project*, trans. Howard Eiland and Kevin McLaughlin. Cambridge, MA: Harvard University Press, 1999.

———. "On the Concept of History." In *Selected Writings, Vol. 4 1938–40*, edited by Michael W. Jennings. Cambridge, MA: Harvard University Press, 2003.

Berkman, Franya J. *Monument Eternal: The Music of Alice Coltrane*. Middletown, CT: Wesleyan University Press, 2010.

Booth, Stanley. "Gimme Shelter: The True Adventures of Altamont." *Criterion*, December 1, 2009. www.criterion.com/current/posts/104-gimme-shelter-the-true-adventures-of-altamont.

Bowman, Rob. *Soulsville, USA: The Story of Stax Records*. New York: Schirmer Books, 1997.

Bibliography

Brill, Lesley. *Crowds, Power, and Transformation in Cinema*. Detroit, MI: Wayne State University Press, 2006.
Brooks, Daphne A. "Nina Simone's Triple Play." *Callaloo* 34, no. 1 (Winter 2011): 176–97.
———. "At 'Black Woodstock,' an All-Star Lineup Delivered Joy and Renewal to 300,000." *The New York Times*, August 15, 2019. https://www.nytimes.com/2019/08/15/arts/music/black-woodstock-harlem-festival-1969.html.
Burford, Mark. "Family Affairs, Part II: Black Baptists and Chicago Gospel." In *Mahalia Jackson and the Black Gospel Field*. New York: Oxford Academic, 2018.
Canetti, Elias. *Crowds and Power*, trans. Carol Stewart. New York: The Viking Press, 1962.
Cocker, Emma. "Ethical Possession: Borrowing from the Archives." In *Cultural Borrowings: Appropriation, Reworking, Transformation*, ed. Iain Robert Smith, 92–110. Scope e-book, 2009. https://www.nottingham.ac.uk/scope/issues/2009/october-issue-15.aspx.
Colbert, Soyica Diggs, Douglas A. Jones Jr., and Shane Vogel. "Introduction: Tidying Up After Repetition." In *Race and Performance after Repetition Performance*, edited by Soyica Diggs Colbert, Douglas A. Jones Jr., and Shane Vogel, 1–28. Durham, NC: Duke University Press, 2020.
Crawley, Ashon. *Blackpentecostal Breath: The Aesthetics of Possibility*. New York: Fordham University Press, 2017.
Darden, Robert. *People Get Ready! A New History of Black Gospel Music*. New York: Continuum, 2004.
———. *Nothing but Love in God's Water, Vol. 1: Black Sacred Music from the Civil War to the Civil Rights Movement*. University Park: Pennsylvania State University Press, 2014.
———*Nothing but Love in God's Water, Vol. 2: Black Sacred Music from Sit-Ins to Resurrection City*. University Park: Pennsylvania State University Press, 2016.
Demopoulos, Alaina. "From Bebe Rexha to Steve Lacy: Why Are Fans Throwing Phones at Musicians?." *The Guardian*, June 22, 2023. https://www.theguardian.com/music/2023/jun/22/music-concerts-fans-throwing-phones.
Dwyer, Michael D. *Back to the Fifties: Nostalgia, Hollywood Film, and Popular Music of the Seventies and Eighties*. New York: Oxford University Press, 2015.
Ehrenreich, Barbara. *Dancing in the Streets: A History of Collective Joy*. New York: Metropolitan Books, 2007.
Finley, Stephen C., Margarita Simon Guillory, and Hugh R. Page. "Introduction: Africana Esoteric Studies: Mapping a New Endeavor." In *Esotericism in African American Religious Experience*, edited by Stephen C. Finley, Margarita Simon Guillory, and Hugh R. Page, 1–20, Leiden: Brill, 2015.
Foster, Hal. "An Archival Impulse." *October* 110 (Autumn 2004).
Gilroy, Paul. "Between the Blues and the Blues Dance." In *The Auditory Culture Reader*, edited by Michael Bull and Les Back, 381–95. Oxford and New York: Berg, 2003.
Hamilton, Jack. *Just Around Midnight: Rock and Roll and the Racial Imagination*. Cambridge, MA: Harvard University Press, 2016.
Handy, Bruce. "Questlove Remembers the Black Woodstock." *The New Yorker*, July 12 & 19, 2021. https://www.newyorker.com/magazine/2021/07/12/questlove-remembers-the-black-woodstock.
Heilbut, Anthony. *The Gospel Sound: Good News and Bad Times*. New York: Limelight Editions, 1985.

Hull, Gloria T. *Soul Talk: The New Spirituality of African-American Women.* Rochester, VT: Inner Traditions Int., 2001.

Iversen, Gunnar, and Scott MacKenzie. *Mapping the Rockumentary: Images of Sound and Fury.* Edinburgh: Edinburgh University Press, 2021.

Jaffe, Patricia. "Editing Cinéma Verité." *Film Comment* 3, no. 3 (Summer 1965): 43–47.

James, David E. *Rock 'n' Film: Cinema's Dance with Popular Music.* New York: Oxford University Press, 2016.

Joseph, Peniel E. "Historians and the Black Power Movement." *OAH Magazine of History* 22, no. 3 (July 2008): 8–15.

———. *The Sword and the Shield: The Revolutionary Lives of Malcolm X and Martin Luther King Jr.* New York: Basic Books, 2020.

Juarez, Kristin. "Within the Whirlwind of the Encounter: An Interview with Okwui Okpokwasili." *Liquid Blackness: Journal of Aesthetics and Black Studies* 5, no. 2 (October 2021).

Keeling, Kara. *Queer Times, Black Futures. Sexual Cultures.* New York: New York University Press, 2020.

Kelley, Robin D. G. *Freedom Dreams: The Black Radical Imagination.* Boston, MA: Beacon Press, 2002.

Kot, Greg. *I'll Take You There: Mavis Staples, The Staple Singers, and the March Up Freedom's Highway.* New York: Scribner, 2014.

Lang, Brent. "Questlove to Make Directorial Debut with 'Black Woodstock'." *Variety*, December 2, 2019. https://variety.com/2019/film/news/questlove-ahmir-thompson-black-woodstock-documentary-1203420841/.

Lang, Michael, and Holly George-Warren. *The Road to Woodstock.* New York: HarperCollins, 2009.

Leacock, Richard. "For an Uncontrolled Cinema." *Film Culture* 22–23 (1961): 23–25.

Lordi, Emily J. *The Meaning of Soul: Black Music and Resilience since the 1960s.* Durham, NC: Duke University Press, 2020.

MacAdams, Lewis. *Birth of the Cool: Beat, Bebop, and the American Avant Garde.* New York: Simon & Schuster, 2012.

McCormack, Derek P. *Refrains for Moving Bodies: Experience and Experiment in Affective Spaces.* Durham, NC: Duke University Press, 2013.

Mezzofiore, Gianluca. "A White Woman Called Police on Black People Barbecuing. This Is How the Community Responded." *CNN.com*, May 22, 2018. https://www.cnn.com/2018/05/22/us/white-woman-black-people-oakland-bbq-trnd/index.html.

Moayeri, Lily. "Actually, the Revolution WAS Televised: The True Story of the 'Lost Footage' from *Summer of Soul*." *Book & Film Globe*, July 29, 2021. https://bookandfilmglobe.com/film/summer-of-soul-lost-footage/.

Morgan, Richard. "The Story Behind the Harlem Cultural Festival Featured in 'Summer of Soul'." *Smithsonian Magazine*, July 8, 2021. https://www.smithsonianmag.com/history/black-woodstock-summer-of-soul-146793268/.

Morris, Wesley. "'Summer of Soul' Review: In 1969 Harlem, a Music Festival Stuns." *The New York Times*, June 24, 2021. https://www.nytimes.com/2021/06/24/movies/summer-of-soul-review.html.

Murch, Donna. "The Many Meanings of Watts: Black Power, *Wattstax*, and the Carceral State." *OAH Magazine of History* 26, no. 1 (2012).

Neal, Ron. "The Black Arts Movement." *The Drama Review* 12, no. 4, Black Theatre (Summer, 1968).

O'Hagan, Sean. "Film Review: Soul Power." *The Guardian*, July 11, 2009. https://www.theguardian.com/film/2009/jul/12/soul-power-james-brown.

Ongiri, Amy Abugo. *Spectacular Blackness: The Cultural Politics of the Black Power Movement and the Search for a Black Aesthetic*. Charlottesville: University of Virginia Press, 2009.

Palmer, Landon. "The Portable Recording Studio: Documentary Filmmaking and Live Album Recording, 1967–1969." *iaspm@journal* 6, no. 2 (2016): 49–69.

———*Rock Star/Movie Star: Power and Performance in Cinematic Rock Stardom*. New York: Oxford University Press, 2020.

———. "Strategies of the Popular Music Documentary's Recovery Mode." In *Reclaiming Popular Documentary*, edited by Christie Milliken and Steve F. Anderson, 259–6. Bloomington: Indiana University Press, 2021.

PBS. "Africans in America | Part 2 | Religion and Slavery." www.pbs.org/wgbh/aia/part2/2narr2.html.

Peters, Art. "75,000 Miss Moon Landing; Rock in Rain to Motown 'Soul' Music." *Philadelphia Tribune*, July 26, 1969, 22.

Petrie, Gavin. *Black Music*. London: Hamlyn Publishing Group, Ltd., 1974.

Prettyman, Michele. "On the Collection: Flash(es) of the Spirit: Images of Black Life as a Spiritual Encounter." *World Records*, August 1, 2022. https://worldrecordsjournal.org/on-the-collection-flashes-of-the-spirit-images-of-black-life-as-a-spiritual-ncounter/.

Price, Emmett G. III. "The Spiritual Ethos in Black Music and Its Quintessential Exemplar, John Coltrane." In *John Coltrane and Black America's Quest for Freedom: Spirituality and the Music*, edited by Leonard Brown, 153–72. Oxford: Oxford University Press, 2010.

Questlove, with Ben Greenman. *Music Is History*. New York: Abrams Image, 2021.

Ralph, Pat. "Questlove Shares How He First Saw 'Summer of Soul' Footage – But He Had No Idea What He Was Watching." *Philly Voice*, July 15, 2021. https://www.phillyvoice.com/questlove-summer-of-soul-film-hulu-seth-meyers-harlem-cultural-festival/.

Remnick, David. "The Gospel According to Mavis Staples." *The New Yorker*, July 4, 2022. https://www.newyorker.com/magazine/2022/07/04/the-gospel-according-to-mavis-staples.

Russell, Catherine. *Archiveology: Walter Benjamin and Archival Film Practices*. Durham, NC: Duke University Press, 2018.

Russell, Tony, "Obituary: 'Pops' Staples." *The Guardian*, December 29, 2000. https://www.theguardian.com/news/2000/dec/29/guardianobituaries.

Sanders, Topher, Kate Rabinowitz, and Benjamin Conarck. "Walking While Black: Jacksonville's Enforcement of Pedestrian Violations Raises Concerns That It's Another Example of Racial Profiling." *ProPublica*, November 16, 2017. https://www.propublica.org/series/walking-while-black.

Sandomir, Richard. "Hal Tulchin, Who Documented a 'Black Woodstock,' Dies at 90." *New York Times*, September 14, 2017. https://www.nytimes.com/2017/09/14/arts/television/hal-tulchin-90-dies-documented-a-little-seen-black-woodstock.html.

Sanneh, Kelefa. "The Rap Against Rockism." *The New York Times*, October 31, 2004. https://www.nytimes.com/2004/10/31/arts/music/the-rap-against-rockism.html.

Sister Rosetta Tharpe. "Up above My Head (France 1965)." *YouTube*, October 15, 2014. www.youtube.com/watch?v=P9BFVeZr5Sc.

Smithsonian Folkways Recordings. "The Singing and Praying Bands of Maryland and Delaware." *Smithsonian Folkways Magazine*, Winter 2014. https://folkways.

si.edu/magazine-fall-winter-2014-singing-praying-bands-maryland-delaware/gospel-african-american-sacred/music/article/smithsonian.

Soul to Soul: Music From the Original Soundtrack. *Atlantic Records*, 1971.

Taleb, Nassim Nicholas. *The Black Swan: The Impact of the Highly Improbable*. New York: Random House Trade Paperbacks, 2010.

The Black Outdoors: Fred Moten & Saidiya Hartman. https://fhi.duke.edu/videos/black-outdoors-fred-moten-saidiya-hartman.

Thompson, Clifford. "'When Black Was Born': *Summer of Soul*." *Commonweal* 148, no. 8 (September 2021).

Tick, Judith, and Paul Beaudoin, eds. "Thomas Andrew Dorsey 'Bring the People Up' and Carries Himself Along." In *Music in the USA: A Documentary Companion*, 404–08. New York: Oxford University Press, 2008.

Tischauser, Jeff. "After Patriot-Linked Vandalism, a Black Artist Searches for Vindication." *Southern Poverty Law Center*, April 17, 2023. https://www.splcenter.org/hatewatch/2023/04/17/after-patriot-front-linked-vandalism-black-artist-searches-vindication.

Tobias, James. "The Music Film as Essay: Montage as Argument in Khalil Joseph's *Fly Paper* and *Process*." In "IN FOCUS: Modes of Black Liquidity: Music Video as Black Art," edited by Alessandra Raengo and Lauren McLeod Cramer, special issue. *Journal of Cinema and Media Studies* 59, no. 2 (Winter 2020): 157–62.

Torlasco, Domietta. *The Heretical Archive*. Minneapolis: Minnesota University Press, 2013.

Tratner, Michael. *Crowd Scenes: Movies and Mass Politics*. New York: Fordham University Press, 2008.

Uroskie, Andrew V. "Far Above the Madding Crowd: The Spatial Rhetoric of Mass Representation." In *Crowds*, edited by Jeffrey T. Schnapp and Matthew Tiews. Stanford, CA: Stanford University Press, 2006.

Vidler, Anthony. *The Architectural Uncanny: Essays in the Modern Unhomely*. Cambridge: MIT Press, 1992.

Wald, Gayle. *Shout, Sister, Shout! The Untold Story of Rock-and-Roll Trailblazer Sister Rosetta Tharpe*. Boston, MA: Beacon Press, 2007.

———. "Soul Vibrations: Black Music and Black Freedom in Sound and Space." *American Quarterly* 63, no. 3 (September 1, 2011): 673–96.

———, and Chester Higgins. *It's Been Beautiful: Soul! and Black Power Television*. Durham, NC: Duke University Press, 2015.

Wexler, Jerry. "'Handcrafting the Grooves' in the Studio: Aretha Franklin at Muscle Shoals." In *Music in the USA: A Documentary Companion*, edited by Judith Tick with Paul Beaudoin, 612–18. New York: Oxford University Press, 2008.

Winston, Brian. *Lies, Damn Lies and Documentaries*. London: British Film Institute, 2000.

Zapotosky, Matt. "Charleston Church Shooter: 'I Would Like to Make It Crystal Clear, I Do Not Regret What I Did'." *The Washington Post*, January 4, 2017. https://www.washingtonpost.com/world/national-security/charleston-church-shooter-i-would-like-to-make-it-crystal-clear-i-do-not-regret-what-i-did/2017/01/04/05b0061e-d1da-11e6-a783-cd3fa950f2fd_story.html.

Contributor Bios

Lauren McLeod Cramer is an assistant professor in the Cinema Studies Institute at the University of Toronto. Her work focuses on the aesthetics of blackness and popular culture. She is currently writing a book on hip-hop visual culture and black spatial practices. Lauren is the co-editor of *liquid blackness: journal of aesthetics and black studies*. Her writing has appeared in *The Journal of Cinema and Media Studies*, *The Black Scholar*, *Black Camera*, *Film Criticism*, *The Los Angeles Review of Books*, *The Quarterly Review of Film and Video*, and *ASAP/J*.

Anthony Kinik is Associate Professor of Film Studies at Brock University in St. Catharines, Ontario. His areas of specialization include documentary film, experimental film, and cinema's complex relationship with the urban environment. Together with Steven Jacobs and Eva Hielscher, he co-edited the book *The City Symphony Phenomenon: Cinema, Art, and Urban Modernity Between the Wars* (Routledge 2019) and contributed essays on Gordon Sparling's 1930s Canadian city symphonies and Ralph Steiner and Willard Van Dyke's *The City* (1939) to the collection. More recently, his essay "Errol Morris, *The New York Times*, and Op-Docs as Pop Docs" appeared in the collection *Reclaiming Popular Documentary* (Indiana University Press, 2021), while "Minimum and Maximum Rock 'n' Roll: Nick Cave and the Bad Seeds and Rockumentary Form" was published in the collection *Mapping the Rockumentary: Images of Sound and Fury* (Edinburgh University Press, 2021). He is currently working on a book on Sixties Montreal as a cinematic city.

Landon Palmer is an assistant professor in the Department of Journalism and Creative Media at the University of Alabama. His research focuses on historical intersections between American motion picture and popular music cultures, which has appeared in *Journal of Cinema and Media Studies*, *Journal of Popular Music Studies*, *Music, Sound, and the Moving Image*, and several scholarly anthologies. He has published studies on concert documentaries as part of his monograph *Rock Star/Movie Star: Power and Performance in Cinematic Rock Stardom* and for *iaspm@journal* and

Historical Journal of Film, Radio, and Television. From 2013 to 2017, he reviewed music documentaries for the website Nonfics.

Michele Prettyman is a scholar of film and African American cinema and visual culture and an assistant professor in Fordham University's Department of Communication and Media Studies. Her research explores Black aesthetic and cultural histories, experimental modes of filmmaking and storytelling, and blackness at the intersection of aesthetics and spirituality. She is a founding member of the *liquid blackness* research project, serving on its editorial board and the board of *Short Film Studies* journal. Some of her recent work includes an essay in the anthology *Black Cinema & Visual Culture: Art and Politics in the 21st Century* titled, "Out of Form Into Being: Black Women Filmmakers and Experiments in Expansive Cinema." Additional work appears in the *Journal of Cinema and Media Studies*, *Black Camera*, *The Lemonade Reader* anthology, and in other online journals. She has been featured on numerous panels, podcasts, and media events working with venerated organizations, including Third World Newsreel, Georgia Public Broadcasting, the Jacob Burns Film Center, and the American Black Film Festival (ABFF). In 2019, she was named Artistic Director of the Tubman African American Museum's inaugural film festival, and she is a co-founder of Daughters of Eve Media, a consulting company that programs film events and provides a platform for storytellers. She appears alongside Chuck D, the late John Singleton, and others in the documentary film, *Oscar Micheaux: The Superhero of Black Filmmaking* (2021) streaming now on Max.

Catherine Russell is Distinguished University Professor of Film Studies at Concordia University in Montreal. She is the author of six books, including *The Cinema of Barbara Stanwyck: 26 Short Essays on a Working Star* (Illinois, 2923), *Experimental Ethnography: The Work of Film in the Age of Video* (Duke, 1999), *Archiveology: Walter Benjamin and Archival Film Practices* (Duke, 2018), and *The Cinema of Naruse Mikio: Women and Japanese Modernity* (Duke, 2008). Her articles on documentary cinema, Japanese cinema, and experimental film have appeared in numerous journals, collections, readers, and anthologies. She is a contributing writer for *Cineaste* magazine.

Index

5th Dimension, The 4, 18, 23, 69–71
16mm 37, 42, 43
1969 Rock and Roll Revival 45n6

ABC Worldwide Syndication 43
Academy Award 21, 45, 48
activism 6, 12, 16, 18, 39
affect 6, 16, 22
Afrofuturism 11–13
Akomfrah, John 7, 12–15
Ali, Muhammad 54, 65
All Tomorrow's Parties (Jonathan Caouette, 2009) 48
Altamont Speedway Free Festival 5n1, 45n6
Amazing Grace (Alan Elliott, 2018) 15, 63n49, 65
Amy (Asif Kapadia, 2015) 61n5
Apollo 11 34, 47
archive 16, 24–5, 26, 31; archival audio 42; archival footage 16, 22, 35, 36, 39, 41, 42, 56; archival images 7, 19n24, 41; archival material 14, 15, 24, 28, 31; archival reveal 23; Black archival impulse 23–6, 29, 30–1
archiveology 8, 12, 15, 19n24
Armstrong, Louis 54
Artie Shaw: Time Is All You've Got (Brigitte Berman, 1985) 61n5
authenticity 4, 35, 36, 37, 38

Baez, Joan 46n12
Band, The 50
Baraka, Amiri 50
Bar-Kays, The 53
Barretto, Ray 16, 23, 30
Beatles, The 38, 50
Bell, Al 52, 53, 58

Benjamin, Walter 6–8, 12, 16, 18
Berry, Chuck 38
Black Arts Movement 4, 50–1, 62n15
Black Audio Film Collective 12
Black concert films 64–5, 72
Black futurism 7, 8, 11, 12
Black Lives Matter 6, 8, 18
blackness 24, 37, 44
Black Panthers 31n1, 50
Black Power 6, 9, 50, 51, 61
Black Woodstock 17, 22, 35, 42, 45, 48, 50, 52
bluegrass 49
blues 10, 11, 14, 34, 36, 49, 60, 74
Branch, Ben 30, 57–9, 60
Brown, James 65

Cavett, Dick 67
CBS 18n2, 21
cinéma vérité 37
Civil Right Movement 50, 51, 57
Clara Walker and the Gospel Redeemers 57
Cleveland, James 65
Clinton, George 13
collection 24–5, 31
collectivity 24–5, 26, 29, 31
community 1, 3, 38, 39, 41–2, 65
concert movie 42, 61n4; concert documentary 35–6, 38, 42, 44
congregation 1, 3, 5
cosmology 66
counterculture 37, 44, 71
crowd 2, 18, 26–8, 30–1, 33n22, 42, 69, 70, 75

Davis, Angela 54
Davis, Billy Jr. 23, 70, 71

Index

Diddley, Bo 38
digitization 6, 14
digitopia 12, 15–16
Dinizulu Dancers and Drummers 16
Dinizulu, Kimati 30
direct cinema 35, 36–7, 39, 41, 42, 43, 44, 45n6
Disney 11
documentary *see* music documentary
Dont Look Back (D.A. Pennebaker, 1967) 37, 48
Doris Day Show, The 56
Dorsey, Thomas A. 59–60, 65
Douglass, Frederick 54
Drake, Dorinda 39
Drew, Robert 37, 43–4
Dylan, Bob 38, 50

Eckstine, Billy 53
editing 6, 7, 14, 16, 42, 55
Edwin Hawkins Singers, The 39, 42, 55, 70
Emotions, The 65

Falls, Mildred 74
Farrakhan, Louis 32n12
fashion 16, 42, 54
Festival (Murray Lerner, 1967) 48, 49, 52, 56
festival films 48, 50, 61n4, 64
festivals *see* music festivals
Filth and the Fury, The (Julien Temple, 2000) 62n33
Flack, Roberta 51, 65
Floyd, Eddie 53
Floyd, George 8
Foreman, George 65
Foster, Hal 23–4, 31
Franklin, Aretha 15, 60, 63n49, 65
funk 34, 60

Garvey, Marcus 54
Gimme Shelter (Albert and David Maysles, Charlotte Zwerin, 1970) 5n1, 38, 44
Gladys Knight & the Pips 18, 29
Gordon, Robert 43
gospel 16, 29, 30, 39–40, 50–1, 55–7, 59–61, 64–6, 72–4
Grass (Ron Mann, 1999) 46n7

Hair 71
hairdos 16, 52, 54

Harlem Cultural Festival 2, 4, 9, 15, 21, 28, 34–5, 39, 44–5, 47, 64
Harlem Renaissance 8
Harris, Bernard 13
Harris, Eddie 65
Havens, Richie 37–8
Hawkins, Edwin 40; *see also* Edwin Hawkins Singers, The
Hayes, Isaac 53
Heider, Wally 53
Hendrix, Jimi 37–8, 67–8
Herman Stevens and the Voices of Faith 57, 73
hippies 37, 71
historicity 24
historiography 7, 12, 16
history 17, 18, 23, 24, 26, 31, 35, 42–3; Angel of History 7, 12, 18; Black history 14, 25, 28, 38
Hulu 11
Hunter-Gault, Charlayne 56, 57, 73

Innis, Cyril "Bullwhip," Jr. 31n1
intertitles 9, 21, 28
interview 13, 28, 30, 37, 41–2, 55

Jackson, Jesse 10, 15, 17, 30, 41, 53, 57–60, 74–5
Jackson, Mahalia 10, 30, 41, 49, 57–60, 63n49, 74–5
Jackson, Musa 9, 22, 39, 45
Jagger, Mick 38
Janis: Little Girl Blue (Amy Berg, 2015) 46n7
jazz 10, 34, 49, 60, 74; free jazz 11, 12
Jazz on a Summer's Day (Bert Stern and Aram Avakian, 1959) 48, 49, 74
Jefferson Airplane 46n12
Johnson, Robert 12
Jones, Jimmy 53
Joplin, Janis 46n12

Keeling, Kara 7–8, 11, 12, 14–15
Kids Are Alright, The (Jeff Stein, 1979) 46n7
King, Albert 53
King, B.B. 65
King, Martin Luther, Jr. 4, 10, 30, 41, 47, 49, 54, 57
Klee, Paul 12
Knight, Gladys 71; *see also* Gladys Knight & the Pips

Index

Kornfeld, Artie 38
Kryor, Adrienne 39–40

Last Angel of History, The (John Akomfrah, 1996) 12, 13, 14
Last Waltz, The (Martin Scorsese, 1978) 49
Lauro, Joe 43
Lawrence, Tony 9, 15, 55
Le Bon, Gustave 33n22
Lewis, Darryl 61n1
Lincoln, Abbey 30
Lindsay, John 10
Little Richard 38
liveness 25, 31, 36
Looking for Langston (Isaac Julien, 1989) 8
Louw, Joseph 30

Mackay, William 76n19
Malcolm X 54, 62n15
Masakela, Hugh 16
Maysles, Albert 37
Maysles, David 37
McCann, Les 51, 65
McCoo, Marilyn 23, 70, 71
memory 6, 17, 23–6, 30, 66, 75
Million Man March 24, 28, 31, 32n12
Miranda, Lin-Manuel 39
Miranda, Luis 39
montage 12, 18, 41, 42, 54, 55, 65
Monterey Pop (D.A. Pennebaker, 1968) 37, 44, 48
Monterey Pop Festival 53
Moonage Daydream (Brett Morgen, 2022) 62n33
moon landing 13–14, 34, 45, 47
Motown 34, 41, 53
Mount Morris Park 2, 3, 11, 47, 55, 59, 60
movie theater 3, 21, 43
music documentary *see* Black concert film; concert movie; festival films; popular music documentary; rockumentary
music festivals 2, 35–6, 38, 43–5, 48, 64, 74; *see also* Altamont Speedway Free Festival; Harlem Cultural Festival; Monterey Pop Festival; Newport Folk Festival; Soul to Soul Festival; Watts Summer Festival; Woodstock Music and Art Fair
My Generation (Thomas Haneke and Barbara Kopple, 2000) 46n7

NASA 13
Neal, Ron 50
Neville, Morgan 43
new age 4, 66, 67, 69–72, 75
Newport Folk Festival 52, 56, 74
Nichols, Michelle 13
Nkrumah, Kwame 51, 62n15

Okpokwasili, Okwui 32n6
Oliver-Velez, Denise 25
Operation Breadbasket 57–8, 59
Operation Breadbasket Orchestra and Choir 30, 57
Operation PUSH 58

Parker, Charlie 2
Parliament Funkadelic 12
Pearson, Joshua L. 7, 14, 15, 16
Pennebaker, D.A. 37, 38
performance 6, 36–8, 41, 64, 72; Black musical performance 64, 66–7, 69, 73; gospel performance 72–3; live performance 21, 30, 36; new-age performance 71; stage performance 36, 37, 41, 42
Peters, Art 34
Philadelphia Tribune, The 34
Pickett, Wilson 51, 65
Pollack, Sydney 15, 63n49
popular music documentary 35, 41, 48, 49
Pryor, Adrienne 70
Pryor, Richard 65

Questlove *see* Thompson, Ahmir "Questlove"

racism 9
Rainey, Ma 60
Rance Allen Group, The 53
revival 59, 60, 64–6, 68–9, 75
revolution 6, 10–11, 31, 54
Roach, Max 30
Rock, Chris 41
rockism 36–7
rock music 35–8, 49, 64, 74
rockumentary 36, 48, 49, 61
Rolling Stones, The 37, 50
Roundtree, Richard 53
Ruffin, David 29

salsa 10
Santamaria, Mongo 23, 30

Santana 51
Say Amen, Somebody (George Nierenberg, 1982) 65
Scott-Heron, Gil 6, 25
Searching for Sugar Man (Malik Bendjelloul, 2012) 61n5
Sharpton, Al 56, 57, 61
Sheila E. 23
Simone, Nina 16–17, 30, 55, 60, 63n48
Sly and the Family Stone 12, 16, 18, 48, 55, 69, 71, 72
Smith, Willie Mae Ford 65
soul 51, 67
soul music 6, 8, 10–11, 15, 16, 49, 65
Soul Power (Jeff Levy-Hinte, 2009) 65
Soul to Soul (Denis Sanders, 1971) 4, 49, 51–2, 55, 61, 65
Soul to Soul Festival 51, 53, 65
Space Is the Place (Sun Ra, 1974) 11, 12
Spinners, The 65
spirituality 66–8, 69, 71, 75
spirituals 60, 66
Staples, Cleotha 50, 52, 74
Staple Singers, The 13, 34, 49–61, 65
Staples, Mavis 10, 30, 41, 49–52, 54–60, 70, 73–5
Staples, Pervis 50, 52, 55
Staples, Roebuck "Pops" 50, 52, 54, 55–6, 59, 60, 73–4
Staples, Yvonne 50, 52, 54, 55, 74
Stax Records 52, 55
Stevens, Herman *see* Herman Stevens and the Voices of Faith
Stone, Rose 16, 72
Stone, Sly 69, 71; *see also* Sly and the Family Stone
Stop Making Sense (Jonathan Demme, 1984) 48
Stuart, Mel 53, 55
Sundance Film Festival 33n26
Sun Ra 11–13

T.A.M.I. Show (Steve Binder, 1964) 49
Tate, Greg 29, 30, 56–7, 72–3
television 14, 25, 31, 43–4, 45
Tharpe, Sister Rosetta 64

Thomas, Carla 53
Thomas, Rufus 53
Thompson, Ahmir "Questlove" 7, 8, 11, 13, 14, 16, 22, 39, 42, 48–9, 56–7, 59, 62n26
time 2, 9, 14, 15, 18; now-time 6, 7–8, 9, 12, 15, 18; temporality 6, 7, 12, 44; time capsule 4
Toronto Rock 'n' Roll Revival 38
Tulchin, Hal 15, 16, 17, 18, 21, 26, 35, 42–4, 48
Turner, Ike 51, 65
Turner, Tina 51, 65
Twenty Feet from Stardom (Morgan Neville, 2013) 61n5
Tyson, June 12

Van Peebles, Melvin 53, 54
Velvet Underground, The (Todd Haynes, 2021) 62n33
video 9, 15, 16, 38, 41, 42, 47, 55

Wadleigh, Michael 35, 37, 38
Walker, Clara *see* Clara Walker and the Gospel Redeemers
Warner Bros. 38
Watts Riots 52
Watts Summer Festival 52
Wattstax (Mel Stuart, 1972) 4, 50, 52–5, 61, 65
Wattstax 53, 58
Weston, Kim 53
Willy Wonka & the Chocolate Factory (Mel Stuart, 1971) 53
Wolper, David 53, 62n26
Wonder, Stevie 2, 9, 16–17, 41, 55, 71
Woodstock 99 5n1
Woodstock 99: Peace Love and Rage (Garret Price, 2021) 5n1, 46n7
Woodstock Music and Art Fair 21, 34–5, 37–8, 45, 46n12, 47, 53
Woodstock: Three Days of Peace and Music (Michael Wadleigh, 1970) 35, 37–8, 41, 42, 44–5, 46n7, 48, 49
WVON 57

For Product Safety Concerns and Information please contact our EU representative GPSR@taylorandfrancis.com
Taylor & Francis Verlag GmbH, Kaufingerstraße 24, 80331 München, Germany

www.ingramcontent.com/pod-product-compliance
Lightning Source LLC
Chambersburg PA
CBHW051759230426
43670CB00012B/2350